Religion and Law in the Czech Republic

Second Edition

Jiří Rajmund Tretera
Záboj Horák

This book was originally published as a monograph in the International Encyclopaedia of Laws/Religion.

Founding Editor: Roger Blanpain
General Editor: Frank Hendrickx
Volume Editor: Rik Torfs

Wolters Kluwer

Published by:
Kluwer Law International B.V.
PO Box 316
2400 AH Alphen aan den Rijn
The Netherlands
Website: www.wolterskluwerlr.com

Sold and distributed in North, Central and South America by:
Wolters Kluwer Legal & Regulatory U.S.
7201 McKinney Circle
Frederick, MD 21704
United States of America
Email: customer.service@wolterskluwer.com

Sold and distributed in all other countries by:
Quadrant
Rockwood House
Haywards Heath
West Sussex
RH16 3DH
United Kingdom
Email: international-customerservice@wolterskluwer.com

ISBN 97890-411-8755-0

e-Book: ISBN 97890-411-8778-9
web-PDF: ISBN 97890-411-8808-3

This title is available on www.kluwerlawonline.com

Religion and Law in the Czech Republic

The Authors

Jiří Rajmund Tretera is a professor and guarantor of courses in Ecclesiastical Law, Canon Law and Religion Law inthe Department of Legal History of the School of Law of Charles University in Prague.

Born in Prague, Czech Republic, in 1940, he graduated from the School of Law of Charles University in 1962 and received his doctoral degree in International Law in 1967. He worked in the field of economic law. Between 1984 and 1989, he secretly taught Ecclesiastical Law to Black Friars in the underground studies in Prague and Brno.

He has been lecturing at the School of Law of Charles University since 1990, becoming an associate professor in 1993 and a professor in 2006. Since 2006, he has been a member of the European Consortium for Church and State Research.

Tretera is chairman of the Church Law Society in Prague and the chief editor of the professional, peer-reviewed journal called Church Law Review (overall there have been sixty-four issues published to 2016). He also contributes to the European Journal for Church and State Research almanac (Editor: R. Torfs, Leuven).

His publications include: *Synagoga a církve kdysi a dnes [Synagogue and Churches in the Past and Today]* (1994), *Konfesní právo a církevní právo [Religion Law and Canon Law]* (1997) and *Stát a církve v České republice [State and Churches in the Czech Republic]* (2002). Together with Z. Horák, he wrote *Slovník církevního práva [Dictionary of Canon Law]* (2011) and *Konfesní právo [Religion Law]*(2015). He coordinated the publication of the anthology *Recht und Religion in Mittel- und Osteuropa, Band 2 – Tschechien*, Wien 2004, in the German language, and contributed to the collections *Czech Law between Europeanization and Globalization*, M. Tomášek et al., Prague 2010, in English, *State and Church in the European Union*, G. Robbers (ed.), 2nd Edition 2005, in English.

The Authors

Záboj Horák is Associate Professor in the Department of Legal History of the School of Law of Charles University in Prague. Born in Prague, Czech Republic, in 1975, he graduated from the School of Law of Charles University in Prague in 1998 and received his doctoral degree in Theory of Law from the same university. In 2001, he acquired the LL.M. degree in Private Law fromthe University of Münster, Germany, and in 2006 his ICLic. degree in Canon Law fromthe John Paul II Catholic University in Lublin, Poland. He has been a member of the Department of Legal History at the School of Law of Charles University since 2002, at the start as an assistant professor and since 2012 as an associate professor. He has dedicated himself to religion law, canon law, history of law and, in the past,to Roman law as well. Since 2015, he has been a member of the European Consortium for Church and State Research. Horák is vice-chairman of the Church Law Society and a co-editor of the Church Law Review, published in Prague.

His publications include: *Církve a české školství [Churches and the Czech Educational System]* (2011) and *Církve a školství [Churches and the Educational System]* (2012). Toge

ther with Tretera, he wrote *Slovník církevního práva [Dictionary of Canon Law]* (2011) and *Konfesní právo [Religion Law]*(2015). He also contributed to the following compilations: *Recht und Religion in Mittel- und Osteuropa, Band 2 – Tschechien*, Wien 2004, in German, *Czech Law between Europeanization and Globalization*, M. Tomášek et al., Prague 2010, in English, *Československé právo a právní věda;da v meziválečném období (1918–1938) a jejich místo ve střední Evropě; [Czechoslovak Law and Jurisprudence in the Interwar Period (1918–1938) and Their Place in Central Europe]*, ed. K. Malý, L. Soukup, Prague 2010, and to the encyclopaedia *Dictionnaire Droit des Religions*, ed. F. Messner, Paris 2010, in French.

Table of Contents

The Authors 3

List of Abbreviations 11

Preface 13

General Introduction 15

§1. General Backgroundof the Country 15

I. Geography and Constitution 15
II. General Legal System 18

§2. Social Factsabout Religion 20

§3. Historical Background 24

I. From the Dawn of History until the Beginning of the Czech Reformation in 1419 24
II. Under Two Ruling Confessions (1419–1620) 25
III. In the Re-Catholicized Hapsburg Monarchy (1620–1918) 25
IV. In Czechoslovakia 1918–1948 26
V. During the Communist Dictatorship 1948–1989 28
VI. From 17 November 1989 until Today 30

Part I. Legal Framework and Sources 33

Chapter 1. Constitutional Position of Religion 33

Chapter 2. Other Legislation with Regard to Religion 35

Chapter 3. Typology of the System 37

Part II. Religious Freedom in General 39

Chapter 1. Individual Religious Freedom 39

§1. Individual Religious Freedom Generally 39

§2. Individual Religious Freedom of Children 40

§3. Right to Change Religion or Belief 40

§4. Right to Opt for Entering the Ministry or Religious Orders and Congregations 41

§5. The Right not to Believe 41

§6. Right to Practice Religious Belief in Institutions Restricting Freedom of Movement 42

§7. Protected Manifestations 44

I. Conscientious Objection 44
II. Ritual Slaughter 44

§8. Limitations to Freedom of Religion or Belief 45

Chapter 2. Collective Religious Freedom 46

Chapter 3. Organizational Religious Freedom 47

Part III. Legal Status of Religious Communities 49

Chapter 1. Formal Status of Religious Communities 49

§1. Registered Religious Communities, Legal Persons Deriving Their Existence Therefrom and Registered Unions of Religious Communities 49

§2. Religious Communities Having a Formof Other Legal Persons 49

§3. Religious Communities Without Legal Form 50

§4. Two Degrees of Registration with Special Rights 50

Chapter 2. Autonomy of Religious Communities 53

Chapter 3. Fundamental Rights and Religious Communities 54

Chapter 4. Contractual Religious Freedom 56

§1. Basic Principles and Terminology 56

§2. The Tradition of Church–State Agreements in the Czech Lands 57

§3. Negotiations on New Concordat Agreement 58

§4. Contents of the Concordat Agreement from 2002 59

§5. Domestic Church–State Agreements 61

I. Prisons 61
II. Military Chaplaincy 62
III. Police and Fire Rescue Services 64
IV. Public Health 65
V. Radio and Television 67

Part IV. International, Transnational, Regional Effects on Religious Communities 69

Chapter 1. International Law Effects on Religious Communities 69

Chapter 2. Transnational Law Effects on Religious Communities 71

Chapter 3. Regional Law Effects on Religious Communities 73

Part V. Religion and Politics 75

Chapter 1. Religious Influence in Politics 75

Chapter 2. Political Influence in Religion 77

Chapter 3. Interaction Between Religion and the State on a Political and Legal Level 78

Part VI. Labour Law Within Religious Communities 81

Chapter 1. Scope of Application of Labour Law 81

Chapter 2. Religious Ministers and Labour Law 82

Chapter 3. Other Church Employees and Labour Law 83

Part VII. Religious Communities and Protections of the Individual 85

Chapter 1. Protection of Privacy 85

Chapter 2. Freedom to Marry 86

Chapter 3. Freedom of Expression 87

Chapter 4. Due Process Norms and Religious Groups 88

Chapter 5. Professional Secrecy 89

Chapter 6. Medical Deontology 90

Chapter 7. Non-discrimination 91

Chapter 8. Penal Law and Religion 93

Part VIII. Church Financing 95

Chapter 1. Direct Financing of Religious Communities 95

Chapter 2. Indirect Financing of Religious Communities 99

Part IX. Education 101

Chapter 1. Religious Education in Public and Private Schools 101

§1. Religious Education in Public Schools 101

§2. Religious Education in Religious Schools 103

§3. Religious Education in Private Schools 103

Chapter 2. Religious Schools 104

Chapter 3. Theological Schools and Other Theological Studies at Universities 107

Part X. Matrimonial and Family Law 109

Chapter 1. Legal Position of Religious Marriage 109

Chapter 2. Legal Position of Religious Family Law 112

Part XI. Religion and Culture 113

Chapter 1. Religion and Art 113

Chapter 2. Religion and Media 114

Chapter 3. Religion and Civil Society 115

Chapter 4. Religion and Public Debate 116

Selected Bibliography 117

Index 125

List of Abbreviations

Abbreviation	Czech	English
A. C.	augsburské vyznání	Augsburg Confession
Art.	Článek	Article
Charter	Listina základních práv a svobod	The Charter of Fundamental Rights and Freedoms (Czechoslovakia, Czech Republic)
CR	Česká republika	Czech Republic
Doc.	Docent	Associate Professor Nominated by the President of the University in Middle-European Countries
ECHR	Evropská úmluva o ochraně lidských práv a svobod	European Convention for the Protection of Human Rights and Fundamental Freedoms
EU	Evropská unie	European Union
No.	číslo	Number
Prof.	profesor	Ordinary Professor Nominated by the President of the Republic in Middle-European Countries
Sb.	Sbírka zákonů (Československo, Česká republika)	Collection of Laws (Czechoslovakia, Czech Republic)
Sb. m. s.	Sbírka mezinárodních smluv (Česká republika)	Collection of International Treaties (Czech Republic)
s., sec.	§, paragraf	Section
subsec.	odstavec	Subsection
St.	svatý	Saint

List of Abbreviations

Preface

We are delighted to contribute to the realization of an outstanding project of world importance, the International Encyclopaedia of Laws, in the area of Religion and Law. Constitutional law, criminal law, civil law, commercial law, employment law and all other branches of law in force differ from one another in many particularities in individual countries of Europe and the entire world. The divergence of all legal branches in individual countries is caused by the difference in development and culture and to a considerable extent also by language. Collation and cognizance thereof is gradually becoming more and more vital for a mutual understanding of the diversity of legal systems and for the strengthening of cooperation among all nations of the world by coming closer together. The given conclusions apply to all legal branches. They are particularly marked in the field of religion law. Dependence on the dissimilarity of historical tradition is more noticeable in this field. In addition, it is compounded by an extraordinary delicacy of issues.

Religion law underwent deep changes in the territory of the Czech lands in the course of the twentieth century; they were sometimes continual, such as in 1918, when the Czechoslovak Republic was founded as a successor state of Austria–Hungary, and sometimes discontinuous, such as after the coup of 1948 or the revolution of 1989. In 1948, the dictatorship of the Communist Party was established, which annihilated the previous Czechoslovak democratic system; in 1989, democracy was restored.

The legal system in the free and democratic state, Czechoslovakia after 1989 and the independent Czech Republic after 1993, has been to a large extent newly conceived in terms of the relationship between the state and religious communities, although it takes account of traditions prior to 1948. Its formation was strongly influenced by the system of human rights as it has developed in the frame of the international community of democratic states since 1945.

A new system of education and research in the field of religion law, which returned to Czech universities in 1990, has evolved. The Church Law Society, located in Prague and having local groups in Brno and Olomouc, plays an important part. Since 1995, it has been publishing a peer-reviewed professional journal called *Church Law Review.* The cooperation with the European Consortium for Church and State Research and mutually interconnected information in almanacs that are published annually by the Consortium, as well as the information in *European Journal for Church and State Research* published in Leuven, Belgium is fundamentally important. After numerous contributions by Czech jurists to English publications, which are frequently cited herein, there is this new comprehensive publication of knowledge of religion law in the Czech Republic, which depicts the legal situation as of 30 June 2016.

We prepared this publication within the frame of the Programme of Developing Academic Fields at Charles University in Prague – PRVOUK 06, *Public Law in the*

Context of Europeanization and Globalization, whose coordinator is Prof. JUDr. PhDr. Michal Tomášek, DrSc.

Jiří Rajmund Tretera and Záboj Horák
Charles University, School of Law, Prague
30 June 2016

General Introduction

§1. General Backgroundof the Country

I. Geography and Constitution

1. The Czech Republic is a unitary state with an area of 78,867 km^2 located in central Europe. It borders Germany in the west, Austria in the south, Slovakia in the east and Poland in the north. It stretches across the territory of historical Czech lands, which, in the course of history, constituted the core of the Czech Kingdom (Kingdom of Bohemia), or rather permanent parts of the Lands of the Bohemian Crown (also known as the Lands of the Crown of Saint Wenceslas). These are: Bohemia in the west, which makes up about two-thirds of the country; Moravia in the east, the second biggest Czech district; and Silesia in the northeast, or more precisely Czech, i.e., southeast, part of former Silesia, the smallest Czech district. The unity of the said historical districts is declared in the Preamble to the Constitution of the Czech Republic by the following words:

> We, the citizens of the Czech Republic in Bohemia, in Moravia, and in Silesia,
>
> At the time of the restoration of an independent Czech state,
>
> Faithful to all good traditions of the long-existing statehood of the Lands of the Bohemian Crown, as well as of Czechoslovak statehood,
>
> Resolved to build, safeguard, and develop the Czech Republic in the spirit of the sanctity of human dignity and liberty,
>
> As the homeland of free citizens enjoying equal rights, conscious of their duties towards others and their responsibility towards the community,
>
> As a free and democratic state founded on respect for human rights and on the principles of civil society,

As a part of the family of democracies in Europe and around the world,

Resolved to guard and develop together the natural and cultural, material and spiritual wealth handed down to us,

Resolved to abide by all proven principles of a state governed by the rule of law,

Through our freely-elected representatives, do adopt this Constitution of the Czech Republic.[1]

2. The districts of Bohemia, Moravia and Silesia used to be (from the beginning of Czech statehood in the tenth century until 1950) independent administrative units, which is no longer so; the Czech state is divided into fourteen regions. Nevertheless, the historical division of the state described above still survives. It often projects into the names of various organizations and institutions and is expressed heraldically in the Large National Emblem[2]divided into four squares – the first and fourth containing the symbol of the Bohemian lion, the second of the Moravian eagle, and the third of the Silesian eagle. The distinction between Bohemia on the one hand and Moravia and Silesia on the other is reflected in the internal structure of most religious communities in the Czech Republic. This is so as well in the case of the largest religious community, which is the Roman Catholic Church. Five dioceses, whose borders correspond to those of the historical borders of Bohemia, constitute the Czech ecclesiastical province headed by the Archbishop of Prague; three dioceses in Moravia and Silesia constitute the Moravian ecclesiastical province headed by the Archbishop of Olomouc.

3. As for the religiousness of Czech citizens, for a long time, since the end of the nineteenth century at least, we have been able to see that the degree of religiousness has been increasing, regardless of denomination, travelling to the east. The least religious part of the state is West Bohemia; Eastern Bohemia is of average religiousness and Moravia and Silesia are the most religious regions.

4. By 31 March 2016, the Czech Republic had 10,558,524 citizens, who are ethnically practically homogenous. About 92%–93% of the citizens are of Czech origin. Unfortunately, it is not possible to use data from the latest official census, taken in 2011, as they are sparing of information regarding ethnicity, mainly because of the fact that a large proportion of inhabitants used the right not to answer questions about their ethnic affiliation. Therefore, the following information is based on previous censuses and on current sociological surveys. The only ethnic group forming a well-marked minority settlement in the Czech population is the Polish minority of about 50,000 people found in the geographically small area of Těšín (Cieszyn, Teschen) in the eastern part of Silesia. All other ethnic groups are finely scattered all around the country. The most numerous of these groups, roughly around 250,000 people, is Slovaks, many of whom lived and worked (in federal agencies/authorities, institutes

1. Constitutional Act No. 1/1993 Sb., Constitution of the Czech Republic, The Preamble.
2. *See* Act No. 3/1993 Sb., on State Symbols of the Czech Republic.

of science and other employments) in the Czech lands and, in many cases, entered into ethnically mixed marriages here, long before the dissolution of Czechoslovakia (1993). Another large ethnic group, also around 250,000 people, is Gypsies/Roma, whose ancestors immigrated to the Czech lands from Slovakia, Hungary and Romania after the Second World War.[3]It is difficult to determine the exact number of Gypsies/Roma in Czech territory, as many members of the minority do not identify with their origin in surveys, declaring themselves Czechs or Slovaks. There is a small group of remnants of native German peoples, especially in the borderlands. As for the immigrants in recent decades, there are Vietnamese and Ukrainian minorities consisting of a few tens of thousands of people each; the former have dominated greengrocery and grocery retail to a considerable extent, while the latter have come to the country to work as auxiliary labourers. Quite a large part of Ukrainian labourers and healthcare workers come from the territory of today's Carpathian region of Ukraine, which was, until the end of the Second World War, one of the lands belonging to Czechoslovakia, known as Carpathian Ruthenia. The inhabitants of that region had shown a hearty relationship towards the Czech lands already in the pre-war era. There was a small Greek group settled in the central part of Silesia, the offspring of children of Greeks who had died in the Greek civil war after the Second World War who were, after 1948, taken in by Czechoslovakia. In the past two decades, several thousands of Russians have moved into the spa town of Karlovy Vary, where they have bought and run numerous spa resorts.

5. To gain insight into the religious situation in the Czech Republic, information on groups of Czechs returning home from abroad after 1945 must be provided. They have significantly influenced religiousness in the country; in particular, they reinforced some small churches (several Protestant denominations and the Czech Orthodox Church). There were about 40,000 Volyn Czechs, the descendants of inhabitants from the Elbe River region and from North Bohemia, who moved to Volhynia (Volyn) in northern Ukraine for economic reasons in the decade after 1860, upon an offer made by the Russian government. Further, there were descendants of a much older wave of emigrants who had fled the country as they refused to give up their Protestant religion. Some settled in central Poland (Zelów parish, near Łódź) and in a few parishes in Lower Silesia (around Wrocław). Another group of Czech emigrants, mainly Catholic, returned from Romanian Banat. Being an ethnic-religious particularity, we would also like to mention the affiliation of more than 40% of the Polish settlement in the Těšín (Cieszyn) region with two Lutheran churches.[4]A large portion of Poles and Czechs in the Těšín (Cieszyn) region together form a numerically significant and well-integrated Lutheran minority.

6. A particularity of the Czech lands is that a smaller number of its citizens live in the country on the one hand, or, on the other hand, in towns having more than 100,000 inhabitants. The majority of citizens live in small- or middle-sized towns. The largest city is Praha (Prague) in the centre of Bohemia (1,246,000 inhabitants);

3. Jiří Rajmund Tretera& Záboj Horák, *Immigration and Religion in the Czech Republic*, in *Immigration, National and Regional Laws and Freedom of Religion*, 37–38(ed. Agustín Motilla, Peeters 2012).
4. Silesian Evangelical Church A. C. and new founded Lutheran Evangelical Church A. C. in the Czech Republic (registered 1995).

taking the area of the entire state into consideration, it is found slightly north-west of the putative centre of the country. The second largest city is Brno in southern Moravia (379,000 inhabitants). These two are followed by Ostrava on the historical border between northern Moravia and Silesia (331,000 inhabitants), Olomouc in northern Moravia (231,000 inhabitants), České Budějovice in southern Bohemia (186,000 inhabitants), Plzeň in western Bohemia (184,000 inhabitants), Liberec in northern Bohemia (170,000 inhabitants) and Ústí nad Labem in north-west Bohemia (120,000 inhabitants).

7. As for language, the country is homogenous. The Czech language, used by all citizens, is one of the West Slavic languages. It has been the language of literature and justice since the fourteenth century. Its standard contemporary form stabilized in the first half of the nineteenth century. The Czech language is the official language of the entire territory of the state, although Slovak – another language from the West Slavic language family, which is particularly similar to Czech lexically, grammatically, and phonetically, and which has had in the Czech territory, since the united Czechoslovak state (1918–1992), the same status as the Czech language – is used at the same time. Slovaks in the Czech Republic normally use the Slovak language both in private and in public; many of them, however, use Czech more frequently. Gypsies/Roma have their own language – Romany (Gypsy) –, which is one of the Indo-Aryan languages; however, they predominantly use the Czech language, only some of them use their own language with one another. In the Těšín (Cieszyn) region in eastern Silesia, the members of the Polish minority make use of their right to have their own schools. Bilingualism in the region is reflected in public administration and in several religious communities, particularly in Protestant ones.

II. General Legal System

8. The Czech Republic is a democratic state respecting the rule of law with a market economy. It is a member of the United Nations Organisation (as Czechoslovakia since 24 October 1945, as Czech Republic since 19 January 1993), North Atlantic Treaty Organization (since 12 March 1999) and European Union (EU)(since 1 May 2004). The fundamental constitutional documents are the Constitution of the Czech Republic (Constitutional Act No. 1/1993 Sb.) and the Charter of Fundamental Rights and Freedoms (Charter). The Charter was originally published as a schedule to the Czechoslovak Constitutional Act No. 23/1991 Sb., which came into effect on 8 February 1991. Effective as of 1 January 1993, the Charter was adopted by the Constitution of the Czech Republic; it was published again under No. 2/1993 Sb. The Charter may be deemed as the second part of the Constitution, which focuses on the codification of human rights.

9. 'Promulgated international treaties, the ratification of which has been approved by the Parliament, and which are binding in the Czech Republic shall constitute a part of the legal order; should an international treaty make provisions contrary to a law, the treaty shall prevail'.[5]This implies that international treaties come second in the hierarchy of rules of law of the Czech Republic, directly after constitutional acts. High

5. Constitutional Act No. 1/1993 Sb., Constitution of the Czech Republic, Art. 10.

on the list of international treaties which are binding in the Czech Republic are: The International Covenant on Civil and Political Rights (1966), The International Covenant on Economic, Social and Cultural Rights (1966), The European Convention on Human Rights (1950), The Convention on the Rights of the Child (1989), and The Convention Relating to the Status of Refugees (1951).

10. The legislative body of the Czech Republic is the Parliament of the Czech Republic consisting of two chambers, the Chamber of Deputies and the Senate. The Chamber of Deputies is composed of 200 members elected by proportional representation in fourteen constituencies. The Senate is composed of eighty-one members elected by absolute majority vote in eighty-one single-seat constituencies of approximately the same area each. The executive is headed by a President of the Republic, elected by the people in a direct election, who is the head of state and the commander-in-chief. The President appoints the Government headed by the Prime Minister. The seat of the Parliament, President and Government is in the capital city of Prague. The system of courts is headed by the Supreme Court, the Constitutional Court and the Supreme Administrative Court, all three seated in the city of Brno. The state is divided into fourteen regions with self-governing status. Lower self-governing administrative units are municipalities. There is a four-tier system of courts. The fourth tier is the Supreme Court in Brno, the third tier are the High Courts in Prague and Olomouc, the second tier are regional courts and the first tier are district courts in circuits smaller than a region but larger than a municipality. There are two tiers of administrative courts; besides the Supreme Administrative Court in Brno, administrative justice is dispensed by specialized benches or single judges at regional courts.

11. In Czech legislation, consistent with hundreds of years of central European tradition, religious communities are called 'churches and religious societies' (*církve a náboženské společnosti*).[6]Both designations are deemed equal, and it is upon the free choice of a religious community to use either or neither of the two in its name.[7]The designation 'churches and religious societies' is used jointly and indivisibly in Czech legal regulations. For reasons of uniformity and compatibility with other publications, we henceforth use the common denomination 'religious communities' (*náboženská společenství*), save the citations of laws.

12. The Czech legal system enables religious communities to acquire legal personality and protection of their names through registration in the register of religious communities kept by the Ministry of Culture of the Czech Republic. A religious community cannot use the same name as another already registered religious community and has to meet registration requirements prescribed by law. A resolution on the registration of a religious community is passed in an administrative proceeding conducted by the said Ministry and can be appealed against in a court. Religious

---

6. For the explanation of origins and use of the two options in Czech legal order in its historical context *see* : Jiří Rajmund Tretera, *State and Church in Legal History*, in *New Phenomena in Law at the Beginning of the 21st Century: Czech Law Between Europeanization and Globalization*68–69 (ed., Michal Tomášek et al., Karolinum 2010).

7. Of the thirty-eight religious communities so far registered in the Czech Republic, twenty-four use 'church' (*církev*) in their names, two use 'religious society' (*náboženská společnost*), and twelve use neither of the two designations. It is similar in the case of several known yet unregistered religious communities.

communities are thereby granted the right to create other entities according to their own regulation. The religious communities have the legal right to have such entities recorded in a public register of juridical persons.[8]Unregistered religious communities have no legal personality, but they are endowed with the full freedom to operate and assemble. Rather unsystematic is the fact that some of them have acquired and still acquire legal personality through registration by the courts of the Czech Republic in compliance with regulations on registered associations other than religious communities.

§2. Social Factsabout Religion

13. The presentation of social facts about religion in the Czech Republic cannot be currently based on any publicly verified statistical data. The affiliation with religious communities is solely regulated by the internal regulations thereof, independent of state authorities. Individual religious communities are registered pursuant to a law, but their members are not. We work on data from a survey conducted by the Czech Statistical Office at the latest census in 2011, as well as on facts, which individual religious communities make public about themselves, and on sociological surveys and literature.

14. State statistical summaries are sparing of information regardingnot only ethnicity but also religious affiliation. At the latest census in 2011, the census sheet allowed the people, in its section on religion, to provide four different pieces of information regarding their attitude to religion with the following outcome (in brackets is the number of respondents who provided information in one of the four groups):

- stating affiliation with a particular religious community (1,463,560);
- claiming allegiance to a faith without stating the affiliation with a particular religious community (705,368);
- stating no affiliation with any religious community (3,604,095); or
- declining to give information on religion (4,662,455):[9]

The large number of those who did not provide any information regarding religion casts doubts on the completeness of the numbers in other categories; it can be assumed that a certain part of both religious and irreligious people find it unnecessary to inform the state of their attitude to religion.[10]

15. Unlike nowadays, quite a precise and objective record of inhabitants with regard to affiliation with religious communities in Czechoslovakia was kept until the

8. It is the third register of juridical persons connected with religion held at the Ministry of Culture of CR. The other two are the register of churches and religious societies and the register of unions of churches and religious societies.
9. *See* the internet site of the Czech Statistical Office, http://www.czso.cz/csu/2012edicniplan.nsf/t/D70024DBA2/$File/ZVCR014.pdf, 19 Jul. 2013.
10. Zdeněk Vojtíšek, Menší ohrádky, více houští*[Smaller Pens, More Bushes]*1 (*Perspektivy* 14 2012).

communist coup in 1948, namely through records administered by local authorities. Said record-keeping was abolished upon the governmental decree of 27 June 1954:

> Unfortunately, this did not mean an increased protection of one of the aspects of personal life because the administrative record of religious citizens, especially active ones, was oftentimes replaced by continuous surveillance by the State Secret Police. The decision corresponded with the then regime doctrine on religion as a strictly personal matter of citizens.[11]

It was in the interest of the then atheistic system to conceal the information on the number of people still claiming allegiance to a religion. Not even after the restoration of democracy in 1989 was the original system of record- keeping reverted to, that time for a different reason, however. The reason was the constitutional assurance of the autonomy of religious communities and the increased protection of sensitive personal data, which membership in a religious community falls into.

16. When surveying the distribution of affiliation with individual religious communities and their mutual numeral ratio, we can work with data acquired in censuses taken in 1991 and 2001.[12]Altogether, there are thirty-eight registered religious communities in the Czech Republic (as of 30 June 2016). Approximately 80% of the members of the religious communities belong to the Roman Catholic Church. According to the Czech Bishops' Conference (Česká biskupská konference), 3,887,400 baptized Catholics live in the Czech Republic.[13]The Roman Catholic Church is followed by the Czechoslovak Hussite Church[14]with about 100,000 registered members in 2007,[15]and the Evangelical Church of Czech Brethren[16]with 87,971 registered members.[17]Tens of thousands are registered with the Orthodox Church in Czech Lands. Both Lutheran Churches in eastern Silesia have more than 30,000 members together. Each of the

---

11. Ignác Antonín Hrdina, *Texty ke studiu konfesního práva III.: Československo [Texts to Study Religion Law III.: Czechoslovakia]*261 (Karolinum 2006).
12. *See* the table published in Jiří Rajmund Tretera, *State and Church in the Czech Republic*, in *State and Church in the European Union* 36(ed., Gerhard Robbers, 2nd ednNomos 2005).
13. Česká biskupská konference [Czech Bishops' Conference] (ed.), *Katolická církev v České republice [The Catholic Church in the Czech Republic]*75(Kostelní Vydří: Karmelitánské nakladatelství 2013).
14. The Czechoslovak Church developed from Catholic modernism. It unites both Catholic and Protestant aspects of worship and teaching with the former Hussite tradition. It was founded as a new Church in January 1920 and recognized by the State in September 1920, though not as a State religion. This Church has used the name The Czechoslovak Hussite Church since 1971. It has a small part in Slovakia, too.
15. *See* http://www.ccsh.cz/dokumenty/665-portret_salajka_opt.pdf, 23 Jul. 2013.
16. Evangelical Church of Czech Brethren is the first unified Church in central Europe. It was founded on 17 Dec. 1918 by the amalgamation of the Czech congregations of the Evangelical Churches of the Helvetic Confession (Reformed Church) and Augsburg Confession (Lutheran). Calvinist influence prevails. Legal order is Presbyterian. The Church is a member of the World Reformed Alliance and The Lutheran World Federation.
17. Synodní rada ČCE [Synodal Council of Evangelical Church of Czech Brethren] *Schematismus[Schematization]*, in *Evangelický kalendář 2013 [Evangelical Calendar 2013]*165(ed., Jan Zámečník& Pavel Šidák, Kalich 2012).

following religious communities has more than 10,000 members: the Religious Society of Jehovah's Witnesses, the Church of Brethren (Evangelical Congregationalists), the Greek Catholic Church, and the Christian Fellowship Church (one of several Pentecostal Churches). As for other religious communities, each of them has fewer than 10,000 members.

17. A long-term development trend observed in all three of the most populous religious communities has been heading towards a decline in the total number of their members. The willingness of their members to declare an affiliation with their religious communities has been decreasing. It is thought that this trend is connected with the diminution of interest of the public in associating in general, which strongly reflects in both religious and non-religious spheres. In terms of attending church services, this downturn is not considerable. At the same time, however, the activity of said three religious communities in the field of healthcare, welfare work, culture and education has been extending, so a large proportion of the public not belonging to these religious communities is affected by the activity thereof.

18. As for smaller religious communities, the number of their members has a growing tendency; in some cases, they grow rapidly. Church of Brethren, Unity of Brethren and two Pentecostal Churches have doubled or tripled their members in thepast twenty years. A large number of religious communities was newly founded and soon registered. Some religious communities of East origin (Hare Krishna Movement, Czech Hindu Religious Society, Diamond Way Buddhism) grow not only by immigration, but also by gaining many Czech members.

19. The Czech lands are frequently seen as a predominantly atheistic, or at least irreligious, territory, especially in journalistic and political reflections. However, sociological findings between 2006 and 2007 show that 'Czech society is becoming a society with a high degree of individualized and decentralized religiousness'.[18]Some sociologists point out a particular feature of the Czech nature, noticeable in many important individuals since the National Revival in the nineteenth century, which is so-called timid godliness. It is religiousness which is not manifested outwardly through pompous gestures but rather is spirit oriented.

20. To conclude our sociological information about religion in the Czech Republic, we present a summary of thirty-eight registered religious communities and their two unions.[19]

Religious communities registered before the effect of Act No. 3/2002 Sb.:

(1) Roman Catholic Church;
(2) Greek Catholic Church;
(3) Evangelical Church of Czech Brethren;
(4) Czechoslovak Hussite Church;
(5) Silesian Evangelical Church A. C.;
(6) Evangelical Church A. C. in the Czech Republic (before 1993: Slovak Evangelical Church A. C.);

18. David Václavík, *Náboženství a moderní česká společnost [Religion and Modern Czech Society]*209(Grada 2010).

19. *See* the website of the Ministry of Culture of the Czech Republic, Department of Churches at http://www3.mkcr.cz/cns_internet/, 30 Jun. 2013.

(7) Orthodox Church in the Czech Lands;
(8) Church of Brethren (Evangelical Congregationalists);
(9) Unity of the Brethren (Evangelical Church of Herrnhut);[20]
(10) Evangelical Methodist Church;
(11) Apostolic Church (Pentecostals);
(12) Unity of Brethren Baptists;
(13) Old Catholic Church;
(14) Seventh-Day Adventists Church;
(15) Federation of Jewish Communities in the Czech Republic;
(16) Christian Congregations[21](original founder: Nelson Darby, Ireland);
(17) Religious Society of Jehovah's Witnesses;
(18) Lutheran Evangelical Church A. C. in the Czech Republic;
(19) New Apostolic Church (Irvingism);
(20) Religious Society of Czech Unitarians;
(21) Church of Jesus Christ of Latter-Day Saints.
Religious communities registered after the effect of Act No. 3/2002 Sb. (the year of registration is given after the name of each community):
(22) Christian Fellowship Church (Pentecostals), 2002;
(23) Christian Community in the Czech Republic (founders Rittelmeyer, Steiner), 2002;
(24) Hare Krishna Movement, 2002;
(25) Czech Hindu Religious Society, 2002;
(26) Centre of Islamic Communities, 2004;
(27) Russian Orthodox Church (Podvorje of the Patriarch of Moscow and all Russia), 2006;
(28) Diamond Way Buddhism Karma Kagjü, 2007;
(29) Vishva Nirmala Dharma, 2007;
(30) Church of the Living God, 2007;
(31) Church of New Hope, 2009;
(32) Word of Life Church, 2010;
(33) Church of Faith, 2012;
(34) Church of Saint Gregory the Illuminator (Armenians), 2013;
(35) Salvation Army, 2013;
(36) New Life Church, 2013;
(37) Church of Oasis, 2014;
(38) Community of Josef Zezulka, 2014.

Unions of religious communities as of the effectiveness of Act No. 3/2002 Sb.:

(1) The Ecumenical Council of Churches in the Czech Republic.
Founded in 1968 and registered in 2005. It consists of eleven religious communities as ordinary members (mentioned above under Numbers 3–13). The Roman Catholic Church (under Number 1) is an associated member. The Seventh-Day Adventists Church (under Number 14), the Federation of Jewish Communities

20. This church is known as Moravian Brethren in English speaking countries.
21. This denomination is related to Plymouth Brethren.

in the Czech Republic (under Number 15), the Salvation Army (under Number 35) and Christian Fellowship Church (under Number 22) are observers;

(2) Military Spiritual Service.
Registered in 2005, it consists of five religious communities (mentioned above under Numbers 1, 3, 4, 8 and 14).

§3. Historical Background

I. From the Dawn of History until the Beginning of the Czech Reformation in 1419

21. At the beginning of our era, Celtic tribes settled in the Czech lands. The Celtic tribe of Boii gave its name to the Latin expression for Čechy – Boiohemium, or Bohemia. After the era of the Germanic Marcomanni settlement between the first and fifth centuries, the West-Slavonic ethnics, pagan at the time indeed, penetrated the territory from the North and brought the entire territory of the contemporary Czech lands under their control.[22]

22. During the ninth century, the ancestors of the Czechs and Slovaks accepted Christianity in the territory of their first common state, the Great Moravian Empire. After a brief influence by Irish and Franconian missions, there was the great Greek-Slavonic mission of two brothers, Saints (St.) Cyril and Methodius, from the year 863 AD, the crucial significance of which is beyond all doubt. They came from Byzantium, but their Moravian ecclesiastical organization was subordinated directly to the Pope; the territory has remained a part of the western patriarchate and western cultural world ever since. The brothers translated the Holy Scripture, liturgical texts and legal provisions into the Old Slavonic language. Their feast day on 5 July is one of the national holidays of the Czech Republic. Their memory is celebrated not only by Christians but also by all Czech citizens, as it reflects the national and cultural self-confidence of the Czech people. In spite of the fact that the Slavonic liturgical language was replaced by Latin in the following centuries, the reverence for the Slavonic cultural beginnings has endured.

23. The Great Moravian Empire collapsed in connection with the conquest of its eastern region by Hungarian tribes at the beginning of the tenth century. Slovakia became a part of Hungary. The centre of the Czech State moved to Bohemia. The Přemyslids, a Czech ruling dynasty, won power over all of Bohemia and Moravia. Prince St. Václav (St. Wenceslas) became a martyr (929 AD or 935 AD). The date of his death – 28 September – is one of the public holidays of the Czech Republic. His memory is celebrated not only by Christians but also by all Czech citizens. The feast is remembered as the Day of Czech Statehood. The Crown of St. Wenceslas – the

22. *See* Záboj Horák, *Religion and the Secular State in the Czech Republic*, in *La religion et l'Ètat laïque /Religion and the Secular State*: *Interim National Reports, XVIII International Congress of Comparative Law/XVIII Congrès International de Droit Comparé,* Washington, D.C.,July 2010, 253(ed., Javier Martínez-Torrón& Cole W. Durham,The International Center for Law and Religion Studies, Brigham Young University 2010).

crown of all Czech princes and kings – has remained a symbol of national independence and unity of the Czech lands for more than 1,000 years.

24. The Bohemian Principality (since 1212 the hereditary Kingdom) was, of course, a Roman Catholic state. It entered into a free union with the Holy Roman Empire. The Czech king was one of the electors of the emperor. After the ascension of the Luxembourg dynasty to the Czech throne (1310), Czech culture was deeply connected with France and other countries of Western Europe. The rule of Emperor and King Charles IV (1346–1378) was the golden age of the Czech monarchy. Prague was the seat not only of the king and emperor but also of Charles University (1348).

II. Under Two Ruling Confessions (1419–1620)

25. Under the influence of Oxford University (John Wycliff), many Masters of Charles University inclined to the Church Reform Movement. The main personality, Master and Rector of the University, John Hus, a Catholic priest, was burnt at the stake in Constance upon a sentence of condemnation passed by the Council (6 July 1415). The Czech nobility protested; masters and preachers persevered with the Reformation, which is called 'Hussite'. Several crusades were sent from all over Europe against the revolutionary actions in 1419 and later, but the Hussites won. In 1436, a compromise between 'Czechs' and the Church was reached at the Council of Basel; 6 July is one of the public holidays of the Czech Republic. The memory of John Hus is celebrated not only by Protestants but also by all Czech citizens.

26. In the period 1419–1620, there were two recognized denominations in the Kingdom: the Catholic minority and the Hussite or Utraquist (Calixtin) majority. In 1485, the Czech Catholic and Utraquist nobility concluded a treaty (The Religious Peace of Kutná Hora). But the hereditary kings of the ruling dynasties (from 1471 the Jagiellons, from 1526 the Hapsburgs) remained Catholic.

27. During the sixteenth century, the Utraquist Church came under the Lutheran influence. A new and small but very active church, Unity of the Brethren, founded in 1457, inclined to Calvinism before the end of the sixteenth century.

28. The Czech Rebellion against the Hapsburgs in 1618 gave rise to the short-lasting free Bohemian Confederacy, led by the Estates Parliament. The political power in the state was in Protestant hands. However, the Rebellion caused not only the Thirty Years War, but also the defeat of the Protestants at the end of the first period of the War, in the Battle of White Mountain near Prague, in November 1620.

III. In the Re-Catholicized Hapsburg Monarchy (1620–1918)

29. The victorious House of Hapsburg began the re-Catholicization of the Czech Kingdom after 200 years of prevailing Protestantism. Protestantism was forbidden, the leading groups being sent into exile. Catholicism was enforced through missionaries from Catholic countries, mainly from Austria, Spain and Portugal. Later, from the time of Maria Therese (1740–1780), the unification of the Czech lands with Austria followed.

The sovereign of the union appropriated the 'iura maiestatica circa sacra'. Consequently, the Catholic Church lost an essential feature of its previous autonomy.

30. Joseph II (1780–1790) issued the Patent of Toleration for his hereditary (i.e., Austrian and Czech) lands in 1781. Two percent of the inhabitants of the Czech lands professed Protestantism, either the Helvetic Confession (the majority) or the Augsburg Confession (A.C.).

31. The process of the separation of the Churches from the State started in 1848. In December 1867, a new liberal Constitution came into effect in the Cisleithan regions of the new Austro–Hungarian Empire. The basis of the Constitution was a secularized state, based on the principle of cooperation with religious communities, and on their parity. The right to be recognized by the State was given to all religious communities that met its legal requirements (1874). The newly recognized religious communities[23]could join in teaching religion in public schools and could offer religious services in the army. The stipends of priests, pastors and rabbis were financed partly by the religious communities and partly by the State (congrua and salary subsidies). The acknowledged religious communities were supported by the State in proportion to the number of official declarations of religious affiliation made to the municipalities.[24]

IV. In Czechoslovakia 1918–1948

32. The Republic of Czechoslovakia, founded in 1918 upon the dissolution of the Austro–Hungarian Empire, adopted the legislation of the Hapsburg monarchy.[25]Children who belonged to recognized religious communities were obliged to attend lessons in religious education in public schools.[26]The Constitution of Czechoslovakia (29 February 1920) assured freedom of religion to individuals.

33. Because the suffering of the people during the First World War was great and the Catholic Church was accused of having too close of a relationship with the Hapsburg dynasty, the position of the Catholic Church became weak in Czech society during the first years of the free Czechoslovakia. The social movement under the motto 'Redress the Battle of White Mountain' caused a portion of Czechs to renounce their membership in the Catholic Church. Approximately 2% converted to Protestantism,[27]11%

23. The Old Catholic Church (1877), and the Evangelical Church of Herrnhut (1880) – nowadays the Unity of the Brethren – known as Moravian Brethren in English speaking countries.
24. *See* Jiří Rajmund Tretera, *State and Church in the Czech Republic*, in *State and Church in the European Union*38 (ed., Gerhard Robbers, 2nd ednNomos 2005).
25. 28 October, the anniversary of the Declaration of Independence of Czechoslovakia (1918), is a public holiday in the Czech Republic.
26. *See* Jiří Rajmund Tretera, *State and Church in the Czech Republic*, in *State and Church in the European Union*39(ed., Gerhard Robbers, 2nd ednNomos 2005).
27. On 17 Dec. 1918, the Czech Protestants of the Augsburg Confession and Helvetic Confession (i.e., Lutherans and Calvinists) unified as the Evangelical Church of Czech Brethren. The legal order of this Church was Presbyterian.

founded the new Czechoslovak Church[28] and a small group of 0.2% converted to East Orthodoxy. Ten percent became non-denominational. In spite of the above-mentioned facts, a total of 73% of the Czech people stayed with the Roman Catholic Church.

34. Most of the Czech Catholics, adherents of different political parties, supported the new State. The main Czech Catholic political party, the People's Party, even had ministerial posts in almost all governments of Czechoslovakia. Some Catholic intellectual centres worked towards the revival of Catholic life in Czechoslovakia, especially in the St. Wenceslas' millennium (1929) and the Czechoslovak Catholic Congress in Prague (1935), led by French cardinal J. Verdier.

35. In 1927, a *Modus Vivendi* was concluded between the representatives of the Czechoslovak Government and the Apostolic See. It concerned the processes for appointing archbishops and diocesan bishops in Czechoslovakia.

36. During the Nazi occupation (1939–1945), Catholics and other Christians in the Czech lands actively participated in the resistance against the Nazis and were persecuted by them. Approximately 10% of the Catholic clergy were persecuted, many of them executed. It helped to rehabilitate the reputation of the Catholic Church in the minds of the Czech public. The Czech nation was determined to lose its intellectual classes, to change to mere 'workers' of the 'Third Empire' and later to be partly Germanized and partly transferred to some eastern countries. The first step in achieving this goal was the imposition of a ban on all Czech universities on 17 November 1939. Some priests and pastors were persecuted because they disobeyed the prohibition to teach university subjects, even at home, or because their preaching defended Christian and human principles and patriotic feelings. Some of them were accused of helping Jews (parish priests often issued false certificates of baptisms of ancestors with the aim of freeing Jews from the racial classification according to Nuremberg Laws and thus save them from deportation to death camps).

37. Most tragic was the fate of the Jews, indeed. There were some 90,000 Jews in Bohemia and Moravia at the beginning of the German occupation. Only about 12,000 survived.

38. Czech Protestant churches and the Czechoslovak Church participated in the resistance as well. Many of their members took part in resistance organizations; the pastors were accused of analogical offences as Catholic priests. Many Czech Catholics and Protestants were imprisoned in the same concentration camps and it was their first school of ecumenism.

39. After the killing of a German Reichsprotektor in Prague by a group of Czechoslovak soldiers arriving as paratroops from Great Britain in May 1942, the terror of occupants culminated. The Czech Orthodox Church priests, who hid the Czechoslovak soldiers in the crypt of their church, were executed, and the Orthodox Church was forbidden. Several Czech villages were massacred. A Catholic parish priest from the village of Lidice accepted a voluntary death with his parishioners.

28. On 8 Jan.1920, the Czechoslovak Church was founded by 150 Catholic priests and in September 1920 recognized by the government. This Church united both Catholic and Protestant aspects of worship and teachings and emphasized the spiritual connection with the revived Hussite tradition. In spite of its name, this Church was neither an established nor a state church, but thanks to the great number of members (almost 1 million) it won a considerable influence in society. This Church has used the name 'The Czechoslovak Hussite Church' since 1971.

40. After the Second World War, democracy in Czechoslovakia was restored according to the doctrine of continuity of the legal order, which was in force until 30 September 1938.[29]Religious communities, including the Roman Catholic Church, became popular in Czech society. Never in history had the number of theology students from all religious communities at renewed theological schools and seminaries been so high. Religious freedom of the time before 1938 was re-established.

V. During the Communist Dictatorship 1948–1989

41. A radical change came after the communist coup d'état in February 1948. All spheres of public life had to accept the 'scientific' ideology (i.e., Marxist–Leninist ideology), which included atheism. Between 1948 and 1989, atheism played the role of the State 'religion'. Religious communities became the only alternatively thinking institutions whose existence was somewhat tolerated. The ultimate aim of the regime was, of course, the entire elimination of all religious communities.

42. New acts establishing state control over religious communities came into force on 1 November 1949.[30]That legislation brought obligatory – but very low – stipends for the clergy, which were paid by the State, regardless of the wishes of the religious communities, as compensation for the expropriation of the economical property of religious communities (1948),[31]and the cancelling of the congrua and other state subsidies (1949). Any religious activity by clergy or lay preachers needed the state's permission, which was granted only for a geographically limited territory. Moreover, the state's permission could be revoked without any explanation. Offences against the Act were punishable by imprisonment according to the provisions of the new Penal Code of 1950 (and later of the Penal Code of 1961).

43. Obligatory civil marriage was introduced in January 1950 for the first time in the history of the Czech lands. This provision lasted until July 1992, when the possibility of alternative forms of marriage (either civil or ecclesiastical) was renewed.

44. During two nights in April 1950, all religious brothers were deported without legal title from their monasteries to centralization camps. Monasteries remained empty, and they were later used for different civic and military activities. This situation lasted until 1990. During the autumn of 1950, the religious brothers were sent from the centralization camps to forced labour units of the army for three or four years and then dispersed as workers. Religious sisters had a slightly different fate. From August 1950, they were deported to camps in remote border regions and were obliged to work outside their vocation, mostly in factories; this state of affairs lasted until 1990. They were not allowed to admit novices.

29. The day of the Munich conference, where the original Czechoslovakia was destroyed by 'amputation of the border areas of Czechoslovakia and their annexation to Germany', *see* Petr Čornej& Jiří Pokorný, *A Brief History of the Czech Lands*56(Práh 2003).

30. Act No. 217/1949 Sb., on Establishing the State Office for Church Affairs (repealed by Act No. 308/1991 Sb.), and Act No. 218/1949 Sb., on State Funding of Churches and Religious Societies (repealed by Act No. 428/2012 Sb.).

31. The State did not expropriate the majority of churches and parsonages, including gardens. They remained the private property of religious communities, without adequate economic basis.

45. During 1949–1950, all elementary and secondary schools and higher seminaries of religious communities (as well as the theological school in Olomouc) were shut down. Clergy training was provided at only three state theological schools (one for the Catholics, one for the Protestants, one for the Czechoslovak Church), with a limited number of admissions. Hundreds of activists from religious communities, particularly Roman Catholics, Greek Catholics, Baptists, Seventh-Day Adventists and Jehovah's Witnesses, were sentenced in fabricated trials to thousands of years of imprisonment in the 1950s. Catholic bishops were imprisoned or interned, too, usually without any sentence. The Greek Catholic Church was expunged in 1950. The Seventh-Day Adventists Church was dissolved in 1952.

46. In spite of the persecution, religious education remained an obligatory subject for all youth members of religious communities at the beginning (which was more than 90% of all children). Perhaps this was showing consideration for some new members of the populous Communist Party who supported the religious education of their children, because they expected it would help to make them 'good citizens'. But it was changed by 'orthodox' Marxists in the Party leadership in 1953. As of that year, religious education was permitted only as a voluntary subject. State administration made an effort to remove it from schools completely, for 'lack of interest'. Children attending religious education lessons were discriminated against more and more. They were denied the right to higher education.

47. Only during the brief period of 'the Prague Spring liberalization' in 1968, and even some months after the occupation of Czechoslovakia by Soviet and other Warsaw Pact Troops on 21 August 1968, was a more liberal regime applied even in religious affairs. Religious training ceased to be odious for that time. The number of children attending voluntary religious education classes increased at that time, and their presence there did not bring adverse consequences upon them. Religious sisters living in the camps in territories near the state border were able to admit a few hundred novices. Furthermore, religious brothers resumed their activity, though they did so only underground.

48. The Prague Spring events did not bring any real legal changes in religious affairs, with only one exception – the governmental decree No. 70/1968 Sb. – which re-established the Greek Catholic Church. The only important change came, even after the Soviet occupation, at the constitutional level. On 1 January 1969, the Socialist Republic of Czechoslovakia was declared as the federation of two States: the Czech Socialist Republic and the Slovak Socialist Republic.

49. From 1971, the persecution of religious communities in all of Czechoslovakia was revived. All religious communities, especially the Catholic Church, became symbols of resistance during this period. They created many underground activities, founded secret religious and lay groups, organized unofficial theological trainings ('flat seminars') and ordinations (at home or abroad), and printed homespun religious literature ('samizdat'). They were supported by some other dissidents, and, many Catholic and Protestant priests and laymen took part in the civic resistance movement called Charter 77.

50. Both the official and underground Catholics organized a pilgrimage to Velehrad, a famous east Moravian pilgrimage spot and memorial to the mission of Saints Cyril and Methodius, in July 1985. About 250,000 Catholics demonstrated their desire for religious freedom. They did it in the presence of the State Secretary of the Holy See and the Czech Minister of Culture.

51. In 1988, Mr Augustin Navrátil, a Moravian railwayman, prepared a petition of Religious Liberties in thirty-one articles. With the consent of the Archbishop of Prague, it was signed by 650,000 Czechoslovak citizens.

52. Many protest events were prepared at the time of the canonization of the Blessed Agnes of Bohemia, the Czech Princess from the thirteenth century, which took place in Rome on 12 November 1989. An old legend foretold: 'After the canonization of Blessed Agnes, the Czech nation will reach freedom.' And the remembrance of that helped courageous citizens, even non-believers, in their efforts to reach the renewal of freedom and democracy.

VI. From 17 November 1989 until Today

53. On 17 November 1989, the fiftieth anniversary of the closing of Czech universities by the Nazis, the communist police brutally interrupted a students' commemorative march in Prague. The events, later called 'The Velvet Revolution', were followed by all of Czechoslovakia. The day of 10 December 1989 may be called the day of upheaval. On that day, the last communist president appointed a non-communist government. He resigned the following day. The Government voted for the policy of legal continuity and of value discontinuity between the new and old regimes.

54. The Parliament repealed legal enactments that were contrary to human rights. The Act of 13 December 1989 repealed the anti-religious enactments of the Penal Code. In January 1990, the legal provision requiring state's permission for any religious activity by clergy and lay preachers was repealed.

55. On 9 January 1991, the Parliament of the Czech and Slovak Federal Republic proclaimed a large amendment to the Federal Constitution, which contained a catalogue of human rights corresponding to those which were guaranteed by international law and agreements. This Czechoslovak catalogue of human rights is known under its inscription,*The Charter of Fundamental Rights and Freedoms.*

56. On 4 July 1991, the same Parliament proclaimed Act No. 308/1991 Sb., on Freedom of Religious Belief and Position of Churches and Religious Societies, which remained in force in both successor states after the amicable dissolution of Czechoslovakia (1993). It is still valid in Slovakia today. The time of its operation in the Czech territory (1991–2002) may be deemed as the foremost period of religious freedom in history.

57. In the Czech Republic, Act No. 308/1991 Sb. has been replaced by Act No. 3/2002 Sb. of 7 January 2002, on Freedom of Religion and the Position of Churches and Religious Societies (Act on Churches and Religious Societies). It is based on the same, unchanged constitutional principles, but it solves some particular problems in a different and more detailed way. The Act liberalized the process of the registration of religious communities and introduced a two-degree registration and the concept of 'special rights' only for the higher degree of registration, which, therefore, limited some religious freedoms.[32]The Act was subject to a reference to the Czech Constitutional

32. *See* below Part III, Ch. 1.

Court. The court's opinion, published under Number 4/2003 Sb., repealed some provisions of the Act (concerning, in particular, the registration of charities and other ecclesiastical bodies) as unconstitutional. But it did not repeal the two-degree registration and the concept of 'special rights'.

58. Between 1999 and 2002, representatives of the Czech Republic and the Apostolic See prepared an international agreement, which was signed by both parties in July 2002. But on 21 May 2003, the House of Deputies of the Parliament voted, by a majority of 110 votes of the total of 200 members, not to recommend its ratification. The political situation was not favourable. The concordat did not enter into force, but it was not repealed. The proposal for such a recommendation may be resubmitted at a more favourable time.

59. Important change was brought by Act No. 428/2012 Sb. of 8 November 2012, on Property Settlement with Churches and Religious Societies and to amend certain other laws. The Act came into force on 1 January 2013. The Act combines restitution in kind of property appropriated from religious communities from 25 February 1948 tothe end of 1989, and financial compensation for non-restored property. It gradually cancels the paying of stipends by the state, thereby introducing the financial independence of religious communities. The Act shall be implemented step by step. The first three lots of land were given back into church ownership in July 2013.

Part I. Legal Framework and Sources

Chapter 1. Constitutional Position of Religion

60. Czech constitutional law consists of the Constitution of the Czech Republic (Act No. 1/1993 Sb.), the Charter of Fundamental Rights and Freedoms and other constitutional laws. The Constitution incorporated the Charter in the constitutional order of the Czech Republic on the date of the foundation of the Czech Republic as an independent state on 1 January 1993 (Articles 3 and 112 of the Constitution).[33]

61. The Charter emphasizes that 'democratic values constitute the foundation of the state, so that it may not be bound either to an exclusive ideology or to a particular religious faith'.[34]We can regard this provision as a defence against the danger of enforced atheism by the state, which was a harsh reality in the period of the totalitarian state (1948–1989).

62. The Charter includes freedom of religion in the catalogue of fundamental human rights and freedoms (Articles 5–16). The enjoyment of these rights is guaranteed to all 'without regard to gender, race, colour of skin, language, faith and religion, political or other conviction, national or social origin, membership in a national or ethnic minority, property, birth, or other status' (Article 3 section 1).

63. Religious freedom is expressly protected by Articles 15 and 16 of the Charter. These articles read:

Article 15

(1) The freedom of thought, conscience, and religious conviction is guaranteed. Everyone has the right to change his or her religion or faith or to have no religious conviction.
(2) The freedom of scholarly research and of artistic creation is guaranteed.
(3) No one may be compelled to perform military service if such is contrary to his conscience or religious conviction. Detailed provisions shall be laid down in a law.[35]

Article 16

33. *See* General Introduction, §1., II.
34. Charter, Art. 2, s. 1.
35. After 13 Jan. 2005, when the Czech Army became fully professional, said provision lost somewhat its inherent importance under peace conditions.

(1) Everyone has the right to freely manifest his or her religion or faith, either alone or in community with others, in private or public, through teaching, practice, or observance.
(2) Churches and religious societies govern their own affairs; in particular, they establish their own bodies and appoint their clergy, as well as found religious orders and other church institutions, independent of state authorities.
(3) The conditions under which religious education is provided at state schools shall be set by statutes.
(4) The exercise of these rights may be limited by law in the case of measures necessary in a democratic society for the protection of public safety and order, health and morals, or the rights and freedoms of others.

64. 'When employing the provisions concerning limitations upon the fundamental rights and freedoms, the essence and significance of these rights and freedoms must be preserved. Such limitations shall not be used for purposes other than those for which they were enacted.'[36]

65. In addition, Article 17 of the Charter, which deals with the freedom of expression, Article 19 (the right to assemble) or Article 20 (the right to associate) may also be mentioned as implicitly protecting the freedom of religion.[37]

36. Charter, Art. 4, s. 4.
37. *See* Jiří Rajmund Tretera, *State and Church in the Czech Republic*, in *State and Church in the European Union*44(ed. Gerhard Robbers, 2nd ednNomos 2005).

Chapter 2. Other Legislation with Regard to Religion

66. Czech legislation regarding religion may be divided into two groups. The first group consists of specialized regulations of religion law, which further regulate in detail the position of religious communities and the religious liberties of individuals as guaranteed by constitutional laws and international treaties (collective and individual religious freedom). The other group is composed of individual provisions on religion, which are interspersed among various laws and other legal regulations providing for other branches of law. The law system is supplemented by domestic agreements between government bodies and religious communities or their unions on their engagement in special spiritual care.

67. Specialized regulations of Czech religion law encompass the following:

(1) Act No. 163/1990 Sb., on Theological Schools;
(2) Act No. 298/1990 Sb., on the Regulation of some Proprietary Relationships of Religious Orders and Congregations and of the Archdiocese of Olomouc; and Act No. 338/1991 Sb., to amend Act No. 298/1990 Sb.;
(3) Act No. 212/2000 Sb., on the Alleviation of certain Property Injustices caused by the Holocaust;
(4) Act No. 3/2002 Sb., on Freedom of Religious Expression, on the Position of Churches and Religious Societies, and to amend some other laws (Churches and Religious Societies Act), as amended by the judgment of the Constitutional Court published as No. 4/2003 Sb. and by other laws;
(5) Decree of the Ministry of Culture No. 232/2002 Sb., to Implement Act No. 3/2002 Sb.;
(6) Act No. 428/2012 Sb., on Property Settlement with Churches and Religious Societies, and to amend some other laws.

68. Legislation which, besides the regulation of other branches of law, contains provisions regarding legal institutes of religion law is described in more detail in respective chapters of this publication. We would only like to mention a selection of the most important ones here:

(1) Act No. 141/1961 Sb., on Criminal Procedure (The Criminal Procedure Code), as amended;
(2) Act No. 293/1993 Sb., on Detention;
(3) Act No. 111/1998 Sb., on Higher Education Institutions;
(4) Act No. 169/1999 Sb., on Service of a Term of Imprisonment;
(5) Act No. 325/1999 Sb., on Asylum;
(6) Act No. 561/2004 Sb., on the Network of Basic and Secondary Schools (the Education Act);
(7) Act No. 40/2009 Sb., the Criminal Code;
(8) Act No. 200/1990 Sb., on Administrative Delicts;
(9) Act No. 89/2012 Sb., the Civil Code, particularly the part which, as of 1 January 2014, superseded Act No. 94/1963, the Family Act, as amended.

69. Domestic agreements:

(1) Agreement on Spiritual Service in the Portfolio of the Ministry of Defence of the Czech Republic entered into by the Ministry and the Ecumenical Council of Churches in the Czech Republic and the Czech Bishops' Conference on 3 June 1998, as amended in 2012;
(2) Agreement of 21 November 2013, on Spiritual Service between the Prison Service of the Czech Republic (Vězeňská služba ČR), the Ecumenical Council of Churches in the Czech Republic, and the Czech Bishops' Conference;
(3) Agreement of 29 June 1999, on cooperation between Czech Radio (Český rozhlas), the Czech Bishops' Conference and Churches associated in the Ecumenical Council of Churches in the Czech Republic;
(4) Agreement of 27 September 2011, concluded by the Ministry of the Interior, the Ecumenical Council of Churches in the Czech Republic, and the Czech Bishops' Conference, regarding the participation of persons in Spiritual Service in the System of Post-traumatic Interventions.

Chapter 3. Typology of the System

70. The Czech Republic is a state in which the principles of non-identification with any religion or ideology, of neutrality, of parity and of the autonomy of religious communities have been applied.[38]

71. A regime of complete (strict) separation of religious communities and the state has never existed in the Czech territory. Nowadays, the state applies the principle of non-identification with any religious community and the principle of parity and autonomy of religious communities, but it collaborates with them in many areas. We may describe it as a cooperative model of secular state.[39]

72. Flat insistency on the principle that the state does not identify with any religion is not only the reception of provisions of international agreements binding in the Czech Republic, but also a reaction to a historically remote experience of the Catholic Church being above the law in the time of a close relationship between 'the throne and alter' prior to 1867, and its weakened form, which lasted until the end of the monarchy in 1918.[40]From a sociological point of view, Catholicism remained the majority religion until 1948. The attempt to eliminate religion in the forty-year period of the Communist Party's dictatorship pushed the Catholic Church in the Czech lands down to a minority position. At the present time, the majority is composed of those who do not profess any creed; therefore, the Catholic Church cannot be talked about as the majority religion any longer, as it is merely the most populous religious minority.

73. The application of the principle that the state does not identify with a sole ideology is first and foremost a reaction to the previous regime. A level of identification of the state with the Marxist–Leninist ideology was so high in the time of the communist dictatorship (1948–1989) that the persecution of religious communities and people of faith can be classified as one of the most severe in the entire Communist Block.

74. The contemporary Czech legal order puts an emphasis on the protection of human rights in relation to religion, inclusive of the freedom to assemble and associate, the freedom of public worship, and the freedom to organize religious meetings, as well as on the protection of both the religious and irreligious provided by the Criminal Code and the Act on Administrative Delicts. To individually redress wrongs done to people of faith, there have been a lot of personal rehabilitations since 1990, namely judicial ones, connected also with compensation for the years of imprisonment or placement into the forced labour units of the army. However, nobody has been compensated for losing a job or an opportunity to study due to their religion. The rehabilitation of religious communities as a whole, started so promisingly in 1990, has slowed down since the mid-1990s and was, at the time of the promulgation of Act No. 3/2002 Sb., overshadowed by tendencies to curtail the development of the autonomy of religious communities. The counter tendency commenced with a judgment of the Constitutional Court of 2005, which stated the obligation of the legislature to enact a

38. *See* Jiří Rajmund Tretera, *Church and State in the Czech Republic*, in *European Journal for Church and State Research/Revue européenne des relations Églises – État*, Vol. 7,306(2000).

39. *See* Jiří Rajmund Tretera, *State and Church in the Czech Republic*, in *State and Church in the European Union*43 (ed., Gerhard Robbers, 2nd ednNomos 2005).

40. *See* above: General Introduction, §3, III.

restitution Act, whereby meeting legitimate expectations of religious communities in relation to their historic property.[41] The efforts resulted in the enactment of Act. No. 428/2012 Sb., on Property Settlement with Churches and Religious Societies. Provisions of this legislation have commenced to be fulfilled against considerable opposition by individuals and some political groups, especially left-wing ones, shown mainly in the media.

41. Constitutional Court judgment of 2 Feb. 2005, file No. II.ÚS 528/02.

Part II. Religious Freedom in General

Chapter 1. Individual Religious Freedom

§1. Individual Religious Freedom Generally

75. In the Czech Republic, the individual freedom of religion or faith is guaranteed by a constitutional Act, which is the Charter of Fundamental Rights and Freedoms. It sets forth in Article 15, section 1 that: 'The freedom of thought, conscience and religion is guaranteed. Everyone has the right to change their religion or faith or to have no religion.' The term 'everyone' means all citizens of the Czech Republic, be them Czech nationals, nationals of other states or stateless persons. The right to freedom of thought, conscience and religion is an absolute right, i.e., it is enforceable against everyone. The right corresponds to the obligation not to interfere with the freedom of thought, conscience and religion of others. The right to the freedom of thought, conscience and religion expresses the incorruptibility of the inner life of an individual (so-called *forum internum*). It obviates any undue influence in connection with thought, conscience or religion, be it exercised by public authority or by other people or bodies.[42]

76. Article 16, section 1 of the Charter of Fundamental Rights and Freedoms reads: 'Everyone has the right to freely manifest their religion or faith, either alone or in community with others, in private or public, through worship, teaching, practice or observance.' This provision protects outward displays of religion (*forum externum*). Unlike the absolute right to freedom of thought, conscience and religion, the exercising of these rights may be restricted by law and solely by law, not by other means (Article 16, section 4 of the Charter).

77. Following the Charter, individual freedom of religion or faith was further regulated in more detail by Act No. 308/1991 Sb., on the Freedom of Religious Belief and on the Position of Churches and Religious Societies, effective from 1 September 1991 to 6 January 2002. It is also regulated by the currently effective Act No. 3/2002, on Churches and Religious Societies, albeit, in an abbreviated form. Only one section (section 2) is dedicated to this individual freedom, while a major part of the law regulates the position of religious communities and their unions.

42. Cf. Jakub Kříž, *Zákon o církvích a náboženských společnostech, Komentář [The Act on Churches and Religious Societies, Commentary]*10–11(C. H. Beck 2011).

§2. Individual Religious Freedom of Children

78. In section 2, subsection 2 of Act No. 3/2002 Sb., it is declared that the right of minors (i.e., persons who have not reached the age of 18) to freedom of religious belief or to be without religion is guaranteed. Legal representatives of minors may give direction to the exercising of this right in a manner corresponding to the developing capabilities of the minors. By its wording, the Act picks up the threads of Article 14 of the Convention on Children's Rights of 20 November 1989, which is binding on the Czech Republic. In compliance with a recognized commentary,[43]the provision shall be also interpreted in the light of the International Covenant on Civil and Political Rights, namely its Article 18, section 4, according to which the parties to the Covenant 'shall have respect for the liberty of parents and, when applicable, legal guardians to ensure the religious and moral education of their children in conformity with their own convictions'. Under current case law in the Czech Republic, there have been no legal disputes regarding the conflict between the religious freedom of a child and the right of parents to give direction to the exercising of that right.

79. Courts have not been addressed to resolve any dispute between parents regarding the concepts of the religious upbringing of their child, and thus the right to give direction to the child's right to freedom of religion, although, such a case may occur, especially after a divorce. Should one parent be granted sole custody of the child, taking the welfare of the child into consideration, the concept of that parent has the main say. However, if the child is placed in joint or alternating custody of both parents, again expressly in the interest of the child, such a dispute may arise.

80. Even institutionalized underage children, i.e., those outside the system of traditional family care, have the right to freedom of religion. Act No. 109/2002 Sb., on the Provision of Institutional Care, sets forth, in its section 20, subsection 1, that a compulsorily institutionalized child has the right to 'freedom of religion, while respecting the rights and duties of persons responsible for its care to direct the child in the extent corresponding to its intellectual powers'.

§3. Right to Change Religion or Belief

81. The right to change religion or belief is guaranteed to all citizens of the Czech Republic. The Charter of Fundamental Rights and Freedoms stipulates that: 'Everyone has the right to change his or her religion or faith or to have no religious conviction.'[44]The same wording can be found in section 2, subsection 1, sentence 3 of Act No. 3/2002 Sb.

82. Under Act No. 3/2002 Sb., no one shall be forced either to join or to leave a church or religious society, or to participate or abstain from participating in religious acts or acts of a church or religious society (section 2, subsection 3). These rights are

43. Cf. Jakub Kříž, *Zákon o církvích a náboženských společnostech, Komentář [The Act on Churches and Religious Societies, Commentary]*25(C. H. Beck 2011).

44. The Charter, Art. 15, s. 1, sent. 2.

part of the right to the freedom of religion; therefore, it follows that they are absolute rights, which 'cannot be in any way restricted'.[45]

§4. Right to Opt for Entering the Ministry or Religious Orders and Congregations

83. In an effort to enforce atheism and eliminate religion, the totalitarian regime took actions against the most active parts of religious communities, i.e., religious orders and congregations in the case of the Catholic Church, and the clergy in the case of both the Catholic Church and other religious communities. Male orders were, inconsistent with the then legislation, eliminated by a forcible action of the state police and the party's militia, and until the collapse of the totalitarian regime they were prevented from the restoration of religious life. Female orders were relocated to police-controlled borderlands; they were forbidden to accept novices, and they were condemned to die out. In the confidential plans of certain governmental agencies, there was a timetable of their gradual extinction by dying out. Admissions for the study of theology were limited (numerus clauses for the admission of applicants, requiring a recommendation by local bodies of state administration and of the party machine). The total number of the clergy was reduced by withholding state's permission to religious practice from individual members of the clergy. In reaction to this, the legislature of the renewed democratic state of Czechoslovakia emphasized the right of everyone to opt for entering the ministry or religious orders and congregations. That means that no one shall be hindered either from entering the ministry or from becoming a religious sister or brother in any religious community. That, however, does not mean that a religious society is obliged to provide an applicant for a clerical (preacher's) or religious vocation with such a position.

84. Act No. 3/2002 Sb. contains a provision regulating this area. Section 2, subsection 4, thereof, sets forth that everybody has the right to opt for entering the ministry or religious orders and congregations and to choose a life in communities, orders or other similar fellowships.

§5. The Right not to Believe

85. Apart from the right to profess any religion or belief and to change religion or belief, contemporary legislation also includes the right not to profess any religion. The no-religion personal status was introduced in the Czech lands by implementing regulations to the Constitution of 1867. Record-keeping of the religious affiliation of citizens was vested in municipalities, and the no-religion status was put on an equal footing with affiliation with a religious community (until 1955). Although, the right 'not to believe' is impliedly incorporated in the freedom of religion, it is expressly stipulated in legislation.

---

45. Jakub Kříž, *Zákon o církvích a náboženských společnostech, Komentář [The Act on Churches and Religious Societies, Commentary]*27(C.H. Beck 2011).

§6. Right to Practice Religious Belief in Institutions Restricting Freedom of Movement

86. Legal orders of states recognizing religious freedom contain special provisions which protect the practice of religion by persons placed in institutions restricting legally their freedom to move. Those are the armed forces, prisons and similar institutions, hospitals, institutions providing residential care, young offenders' institutions, institutions for the temporary stay of immigrants, and asylum seekers. Such legal regulation exists in the Czech Republic as well. It is quite detailed as far as the army and prison services are concerned. In addition to legislation regulating the two areas, there are binding domestic agreements regarding spiritual service concluded by respective authorities and the Ecumenical Council of Churches in the Czech Republic and the Czech Bishops' Conference (with regard to the army, the agreement was concluded in 1998 and amended in 2012; as for the prison service, the first agreement of 1994 was superseded by a second one in 1999, a third one in 2008 and a fourth one in 2013). Regarding the areas of health and social service, there is legislation in principle which still remains to be finished.

87. In the Army of the Czech Republic and other armed forces, no one's freedom of religion may be restricted, be them soldiers by profession or those who either have been called upon to go on exercises by draft, or those who have been mobilized during wartime. No one shall be coerced into either accepting a religion or renouncing it. No one shall be prevented from the exercise of religious activity, and everyone is entitled to have their own religious literature and prayer aids. As for church service and religious ceremonies, a soldier may attend them provided it does not hamper an important interest of the military service. The soldier attends religious services in his free time and usually outside the military area; however, he may attend in the military area as well. Religious services in the military area are conducted by military chaplains, i.e., soldiers by profession, who have been appointed to the service by registered religious communities holding a corresponding special right, and who have been sent there upon a joint recommendation of the Ecumenical Council of Churches in the Czech Republic and the Czech Bishops' Conference in compliance with an agreement these unions, or bodies of religious communities, concluded with the Ministry of Defence in 1998, as amended in 2012. Owing to the requirements of the commanding officers of individual armed forces, the number of ministers whose appointment into the army the Ministry requests increased in the time of peace from twenty-five to forty-three. Practicalities are overseen by the Military Spiritual Service since 2005, consisting of five religious communities, basically those which have so far sent their ministers into the army as military chaplains.

88. The right to religious freedom and its practice is also enjoyed by people serving a sentence of imprisonment, people in custody and people in detention facilities. The right of inmates to attend services and religious meetings and to keep religious/spiritual literature is guaranteed. In addition, no one shall be arbitrarily denied contact with a minister and no one shall be forced into talking to one. Only religious communities registered with a corresponding special right may provide spiritual care in prisons. This care is performed by persons authorized, thereto, by a religious community; some of them do so as employees of the Prison Service of the Czech Republic, and they are referred to as prison chaplains who altogether make up a single body, regardless of denomination, known as the Ecumenical Prison Chaplaincy. This body is connected with Prison Spiritual Care, an extra-denominational civil association, whose members volunteer to care for individual prisoners and visit prisons and detention facilities at least twice a month. Both organizations serve prisoners regardless of denomination; which service is used is up to the inmate.

89. Act No. 372/2011 Sb., on Healthcare Services and Conditions for providing them, stipulates that an inpatient is entitled to the provision of spiritual care by any registered religious community. The patient may not be denied a visit by a minister, should he be in danger of life or if facing serious damage to health. The same year, 2011, an association of Hospital Chaplains was set up. In 2012, an Association of Catholic Hospital Chaplains was set up. Some religious communities have appointed hospital chaplains for individual hospitals.

90. As for healthcare institutes and residential care homes, many of them have been founded by religious communities, namely by Catholic charities and evangelical diaconias, since 1990. These institutes provide care to anyone, regardless of denomination; religious hospitals do the same.[46]However, legislation safeguarding the provision of spiritual care in all such institutes, be them religious or not, is yet to be adopted.

91. Freedom of religion and spiritual care in residential institutions, such as orphanages or apprenticeship and secondary education boarding schools, has not been, heretofore, regulated by a special law. The only regulation providing for this matter so far has been Act No. 109/2002 Sb., on the Provision of Institutional Education or Protective Education at School Facilities and on Preventative Educational Care at School Facilities. The Act imposes an obligation on such facilities to create conditions for the attendance of children in religious education classes and religious ceremonies, or for keeping the religious tradition in accordance with the child's interest and taking the previous family upbringing and intellectual powers of the child into account.

92. Similarly, the legal regulation of religious freedom and spiritual care in facilities for the temporary residence of immigrants and asylum seekers is mainly based on the provisions of the Charter of Fundamental Rights and Freedoms and on international treaties binding in the Czech Republic. Under Article 4 of the Convention on the Status of Refugees of 1951, published under No. 208/1993 Sb., parties to the convention undertake 'to accord to refugees within their territories treatment at least as favourable as that accorded to their nationals with respect to freedom of the practice of religion and freedom as regards the religious education of their children'.

93. A special legal regulation regarding illegal immigrants can be found in section 141 of Act No. 326/1999 Sb., on the Residence of Foreigners in the Territory of the Czech Republic. The religious preferences of foreigners should also be taken

46. A religious hospital providing wide-ranging care in a variety of branches of medicine is the hospital of The Sisters of Mercy of St. Charles Borromeo in Prague, established by the monastic congregation of the same name. Other religious hospitals can be found in Kroměříž and Vizovice in Moravia.

into account in detention facilities, where they are held before they are banished from the country.[47]

§7. Protected Manifestations

I. Conscientious Objection

94. Freedom of expression of religion or belief is firmly connected with the issue of conscientious objection, which is to be understood as the refusal to fulfil obligations imposed by provisions of positive law or by public authorities with reference to inconsistencies with one's conscience. Such refusal manifests the supremacy of moral law or conscience over a command of positive law.

95. In the Czech legal order, the issue of conscientious objection is reflected in the possibility to refuse to serve in the army, which is guaranteed constitutionally. Under Article 14, section 3 of the Charter, 'no one may be compelled to perform military service if such is contrary to his conscience or religious conviction'.[48]Detailed provisions are laid down in Act No. 585/2004 Sb., on Compulsory Military Service and its Ensuring, which was adopted with the introduction of the professional Czech Army. Czech nationals over 18 years of age are still liable for conscription, which includes an obligation to undergo the recruitment process and perform emergency military service in times of emergency or war. Such service may be refused upon conscientious objection within the period of fifteen days of the date of delivery of a decision on fitness for military service to a national, or of the date of declaration of a state of emergency or war.

96. Another conscientious objection recognized by the Czech legal order is the right of medical staff to refuse the rendering of healthcare service if it is inconsistent with their conscience or religious convictions. The application of said objection is regulated by Act No. 372/2011 Sb., on Healthcare Services and Conditions for providing them.

II. Ritual Slaughter

97. A general rule concerning the slaughter of livestock for meat set in Act No. 246/1992 Sb., on the Protection of Animals against Cruelty, is supplemented with an exception for religious communities whose rules prescribe different methods of

---

47. Jiří Rajmund Tretera, Záboj Horák, *Immigration and Religion in the Czech Republic*, in *Immigration, National and Regional Laws and Freedom of Religion*42–43(ed., Agustín Motilla,Peeters 2012).

48. In the legal order of Communist Czechoslovakia (1948–1989), conscientious objection was not accepted. In practice, persons refusing to perform compulsory military service based on conscientious objection, typically Jehovah's Witnesses, were harshly punished. It was the Constitutional Court, established in 1991, that helped to rehabilitate them. *See* the judgment of the Constitutional Court, file No. II.ÚS 285/97, of 7 Oct. 1998.

slaughter. Any exceptions shall be granted by the Ministry of Agriculture. A religious community may carry out such slaughter strictly in accordance with veterinary conditions set by bodies of the State Veterinary Administration for a particular facility. The slaughter shall be performed by a person qualified thereto, who is obliged to ensure the least possible suffering of a slaughtered animal.

§8. Limitations to Freedom of Religion or Belief

98. The basis for limitations to freedom of religion or belief is Article 16, section 4 of the Charter of Fundamental Rights and Freedoms, which stipulates:

> The exercise of these rights may be limited by law in the case of measures necessary in a democratic society for the protection of public safety and order, health and morals, or the rights and freedoms of others.

99. Religious communities are further restricted by certain provisions of Act No. 3/2002 Sb., on Churches and Religious Societies; section 5, for example, bans the formation and practice of dangerous religious communities. Under section 22, subsection 1, letter c thereof, the Ministry of Culture is allowed to commence proceedings on the cancellation of the registration of religious communities or their unions, should they carry out activities contradicting the legal order. The fact that a religious community does not gain legal personality earlier than after qualifying for the registration, completing an application therefor and being truly registered, may be deemed as a certain restriction, although understandable.

Chapter 2. Collective Religious Freedom

100. While individual religious freedom was emphasized even in the pre-war era (e.g., in the Constitution of the Czechoslovak Republic of 29 February 1920), the same emphasis began to be put on the collective religious freedom in recent Czechoslovak and Czech legal regulations, i.e., after the revolution in 1989.

101. The Charter of Fundamental Rights and Freedoms contains several provisions which make the collective exercising of religious freedom possible. In its Article 16, section 1, the Charter declares that 'everyone has the right to freely manifest their religion or faith, either alone or in community with others'. The Charter was clearly inspired by international instruments on human rights, regardless of their effectiveness in the Czech Republic at the time of its publication.

102. The International Covenant on Civil and Political Rights of 1966 contains a similar provision on the collective exercising of religious freedom in Article 18, section 1. The convention, binding in the Czech Republic since the day of its formal adhesion thereto, i.e., since 23 March 1976, was not respected during the time of the communist regime. As is typical of totalitarian states, international treaties regarding human rights were not taken seriously. Provisions of said convention were put into practice after the 1989 revolution. The convention was further reinforced by Act No. 23/1991 Sb., introducing the Charter of Fundamental Rights and Freedoms, which stipulated that international treaties on human rights and fundamental freedoms that are binding in the Czech Republic have supremacy over laws.

103. The European Convention on the Protection of Human Rights and Fundamental Freedoms of 1950, binding in Czechoslovakia since 18 March 1992, lays down in Article 9, section 1 that everyone has the right to manifest their religious belief or convictions 'alone or in community with others' too.

104. The collective religious freedom is also protected by Article 16, section 2 of the Charter of Fundamental Rights and Freedoms, according to which religious communities 'govern their own affairs; in particular they establish their own bodies and appoint their own clergy, as well as found religious orders and other church institutions, independent of state authorities'.

105. Act No. 3/2002 Sb., on Churches and Religious Societies, expressly declares the right of anyone to freely manifest their religion or faith, alone or in community with others (section 2, subsection 1).

Chapter 3. Organizational Religious Freedom

106. In the Czech Republic, religious communities are allowed to freely associate. In this respect, a principal provision can be found in Article 16, section 2 of the Charter of Fundamental Rights and Freedoms, which reads:

> Churches and religious societies govern their own affairs; in particular, they establish their own bodies and appoint their own clergy, as well as found religious orders and other church institutions, independent of state authorities.

107. Said provision is a reaction to anti-religious legislation of the communist totalitarian regime in Czechoslovakia (1948–1989). It introduces the autonomy of religious communities. The phrase 'in particular' is a demonstrative, not enumerative, list of rights held by religious communities to govern their own affairs independently of state authorities.

108. Act No. 3/2002 Sb. also contains, in its section 4, general guarantees of organizational freedom of religious communities. After all, the existence of the law itself is the expression of a wish of the Czech legislature to enable the creation of a special legal form, which the registered religious communities are, and which reflects the differentness of religious communities from other citizens' associations with regard to the purpose of their existence.

109. An important part of the organizational freedom is the right of religious communities to establish something other than strictly religious institutions, particularly welfare and healthcare organizations, called charities and diaconias. That is the area which, at the phases of preparation and adoption of a new law on churches and religious societies, caused conflicts in the conception of the freedom among various political movements in the then society. The freedom of religious communities to establish organizations other than religious institutions, guaranteed until then by Act No. 308/1991 Sb., was threatened by the wording of a provision contained in section 6, subsection 2 of the original Act No. 3/2002 Sb. Under that provision, the Ministry of Culture, being the body that administers a register of legal persons deriving their existence from religious communities, should have a record only of those whose purpose is the organizing, worshipping and spreading of religious faith. The application of that provision would have meant the separation of charities and diaconias from religious communities, and thereby their dissolution, as the law did not allow for their transformation into secular organizations. The contentious issue was resolved in the same year by a judgment of the Constitutional Court of 27 November 2002, published under number 4/2003 Sb. Although the Constitutional Court rejected a motion of complainants, a group of twenty-one Senators of the Parliament of the Czech Republic, for a full repeal of the law, reasoning that merely lowering the standard of religious freedoms is not contrary to the effective constitutional order, it still repealed four provisions of the law, which it had found unconstitutional, *inter alia* also section 6, subsection 2. In the reasoning of the judgment, the Constitutional Court provides a constitutionally conformist interpretation of the law. It characterizes the religious communities as follows:

the mission of these entities shall by no means be reduced to mere worship of a certain religious faith .... but their activity is substantially wider and lies also in the spreading of religious values outwardly, not solely through religious activity, but also through, for example, charity, or through humanitarian or general educational activity.

110. Religious communities participate in general educational activities, besides other things, by the establishing of schools of all types and levels which are a recognized part of the educational system in the Czech Republic. They also set up their own science and art facilities which contribute significantly to research and cultural activities.

Part III. Legal Status of Religious Communities

Chapter 1. Formal Status of Religious Communities

§1. Registered Religious Communities, Legal Persons Deriving Their Existence Therefrom and Registered Unions of Religious Communities

111. In the Czech Republic, we must first distinguish between religious entities per se (i.e., religious communities referred to as 'churches and religious societies' in legal texts) and other religious entities *deriving* their legal personality from the religious entities per se (e.g., parishes; dioceses; monasteries and priories; church lay, clerical and mixed organizations; charities or diaconias). The former (religious communities) acquire legal personality through state registration in a special register administered by the Ministry of Culture. The latter (derived legal persons) gain legal personality upon the creation of a registered religious community in compliance with the regulations set forth by the founding community.[49]These legal persons derived from the religious communities are recorded in another register, administered by the Ministry of Culture, upon the request of the religious community which founded them.

112. The registered religious communities in the Czech Republic can associate into 'unions of churches and religious societies'. These unions obtain legal personality upon a state registration in a special register (i.e., the third register of such a type administered by the Ministry of Culture). The unions do not have the right to establish other legal persons.

§2. Religious Communities Having a Formof Other Legal Persons

113. Up to the present time (2016), thirty-eight religious communities have been registered in the Czech Republic, and the registration of a single one has not been revoked so far. However, there are some other religious communities which have not used the opportunity to be registered as a religious community, the reason being either

49. *See* Jiří Rajmund Tretera, *Religious Entities as Legal Persons – Czech Republic*, in *Churches and Other Religious Organisations as Legal Persons*55(ed., Lars Friedner,Peeters 2007).

the fact that at least 300 persons of age residing in the Czech Republic have not yet claimed allegiance to them, which is a registration requirement, or their own reasons. Some of them have made use of the freedom to associate and have been registered by the courts of the Czech Republic as registered associations, acquiring legal personality thereby.

§3. Religious Communities Without Legal Form

114. Individual religious communities can exist having no legal form. However, should they need to act publicly, e.g., in order to lease a chapel or the like, they are represented by an individual.

§4. Two Degrees of Registration with Special Rights

115. The introduction of the term *registration* of religious communities in 1991 was preceded by the usage of the term *recognition* of a religious community by the state (until 1949), or of the term state *permission* to the activity of a religious community (between 1949 and 1991). A religious community was recognized either directly by operation of law or upon a decision of competent ministry under Act No. 68/1874 of the Imperial Law Gazette (Reichsgesetzblatt – RGBl), on the Legal Recognition of Religious Communities, which remained in force until 1 November 1949. In the period between 1 November 1949 and 1 September 1991, a competent ministry or government granted its permission to the activity of other not yet recognized religious communities through a decision given *praeter legem* ('outside of the law').

116. The term *registration* of religious communities was introduced by Act No. 308/1991 Sb., on Freedom of Religious Belief and on the Position of Churches and Religious Societies, as of the date of its effect, i.e., 1 September 1991. The Act said that all religious communities carrying out activities in the state territory, be it by operation of law or upon the state's approval, shall be deemed as registered. A list of such communities was given in the attachment to the Act, which was an integral part thereof. The list was divided into two parts corresponding with the two Member States of the Czechoslovak Federation. The list regarding the Czech Republic included nineteen religious communities. The Act set forth common rules for the registration of other religious communities in the Member States of the federation. Decisions on other conditions of the registration, e.g., numerical qualification for the application for registration, were vested in legislative bodies of respective Member States of the federation. The then legislative body of the Czech Republic, i.e., the Czech National Council, adopted Act No. 161/1992 Sb., which set the condition in the Czech Republic that a religious community applying for registration shall have at least 10,000 persons of age with permanent residency in the Czech Republic who declare their affiliation therewith, or 500 of such persons if the church is a member of the World Council of Churches. The provision stipulating that 500 persons is sufficient in the case of churches that are members of the World Council of Churches was unfortunate; it led to a misconception that the Czech Republic 'favours' Christian churches. It was a misconception because not only has such a situation never occurred, but also because it was unlikely to ever occur. Hardly ever would it happen that a foreign national church that is a member of the World Council of Churches would have more than 500 adult members in the territory of the Czech Republic. Should members of several national churches of the same denomination (e.g., Anglican) unite and create a new church in the Czech Republic, such a church would probably have more than 500 adult members, but it would not be a member of the World Council of Churches. And should such a new church be formed by the splitting of a group of members from an existing church active in the territory, it cannot be assumed that such a church would, shortly afterward, be accepted as a member of the World Council of Churches. Therefore, the provision was a pointless verbal declaration.[50]

117. There were two religious communities registered under Act No. 308/1991 Sb. in the Czech Republic which attached 10,000 signatures of persons claiming affiliation, therewith, to the application for registration filed at the Ministry of Culture. These were the Religious Society of Jehovah's Witnesses (1993) and the Lutheran Evangelical Church A. C. in the Czech Republic (1995), which, shortly before, had split from the Silesian Evangelical Church A. C.

118. The said regulation regarding the numerical qualification was criticized by both the domestic and the foreign public. The number of 10,000 persons was found to be far too high; doubling the numerical qualification was then found to be a violation of the principle of parity. Said criticism was taken into consideration in the preparation of new legislation on churches and religious societies commenced by the Czech government in 1999. The new proposed legislation combined two contradictory tendencies: it inclined towards the limitation of extensive religious freedoms on the one hand and towards the liberalization of the registration process on the other. The legislature attempted to find a way out of the dual, contradictory approach by introducing a two-degree registration. It extended the access of numerically small religious communities to the registration by reducing the numerical qualification to 300 persons of age claiming affiliation with the applying religious community and residing permanently in the Czech Republic. At the same time, it took out certain rights of religious communities from the existing common ones, and newly created 'special rights' therefrom, which are granted to particular religious communities, namely to those which are 'registered with special rights'. Although, the Act solely uses the term given in the previous sentence, such registration is actually a second-degree registration. Rights that have been common so far have become special rights.

119. A motion for the grant of special rights may be filed by a registered religious community which has held, on the date of filing, the first-degree registration for at least ten years, which has made public its annual report on activities for at least ten years prior to the date of filing, which has duly met its obligations to the state and third persons and which proves that there are, based on the latest census, at least 0.1% of adult nationals or foreigners permanently residing in the Czech Republic who claim

50. *See* Jiří Rajmund Tretera, *Zákon o církvích a náboženských společnostech a rozvoj českého konfesního práva na počátku 21. století[The Act on Churches and Religious Societies and the Development of Czech Religion Law at the Beginning of the 21st Century]*, in *Nové jevy v právu na počátku 21. století [New Phenomena in Law at the Beginning of the 21st Century]*241 (ed., Karel Malý, Michal Tomášek et al. Karolinum 2009).

affiliation therewith. Currently, the qualifying number is 10,436 persons. The attachment to Act No. 3/2002 Sb. lists twenty-one religious communities registered by the state in compliance with the present legal regulations. These religious communities acquired the authority to exercise special rights to the extent to which they exercised them on the date of effectiveness of Act No. 3/2002 Sb. Not all of them acquired all special rights. Out of seventeen religious communities registered under Act No. 3/2002 Sb. between 2002 and 2016, not a single one has yet been granted special rights.

120. Special rights encompass the following: the right to teach religious education at public schools; the right to authorize persons engaged in spiritual care to carry it out in the armed forces, prisons and similar facilities; the right to solemnize religious marriages with civil-law effects; the right to establish church schools as a special type of school different from private schools with public rights; the right of the clergy to confidentiality in connection with the seal of confession or the like, providing the obligation to keep information confidential has been a traditional part of the teachings of their religious community for not less than fifty years.

121. Act No. 3/2002 Sb. has further stipulated a special right to state subsidies to the wages of the clergy based on a special regulation, which was, though it seems like a paradox, Act No. 218/1949 Sb., on the Economic Security of Churches and Religious Societies by the State, adopted at the time of communist dictatorship after the religious communities had been dispossessed of economic property and their right to congrua (supplements to the wages of the clergy) was cancelled. The provision on this special right was repealed by Act No. 428/2012 Sb., on Property Settlement with Churches and Religious Societies, which lays down the process of partial restitution of the above-mentioned economic property and its partial compensation; it has further repealed Act No. 218/1949 Sb., thereby creating conditions for the future financial independence of the state of all religious communities in the Czech Republic.

Chapter 2. Autonomy of Religious Communities

122. No sooner than after the restoration of the democratic legal order in Czechoslovakia in 1989 was the term *autonomy*, designating a feature pertaining to religious communities, used for the first time in the history of the Czech lands. This autonomy means the right of religious communities to make their own regulations, independent of the state and its bodies. It is in the Charter, namely in Article 16, section 2, which says that churches and religious societies 'govern their own affairs; in particular, they establish their own bodies and appoint their own clergy, as well as found religious orders and other church institutions, independent of state authorities'. Act No. 3/2002 Sb., in section 4, subsection 3 expands on the said constitutional Act:

> Churches and religious societies govern their own affairs; in particular they establish and dissolve their own bodies, appoint and dismiss their own clergy, and set up and dissolve church and other institutions in compliance with their own regulations, independent of state authorities.

Said act refers to the regulations of religious communities in many other places, and the wording of the law implies that religious communities are regarded as organizations regulated by their own independent legal systems, i.e., autonomous systems.

123. The principle of the autonomy of religious communities and their legal systems benefits all religious communities, regardless of whether or not they are registered by the state. The principle of autonomy is not inconsistent with the registration condition which requires that the religious community present, *inter alia*, theso-called basic document, i.e., a statement of the most fundamental provisions of the legal order of the respective religious community.[51] A state body is not, as a matter of fact, authorized to interfere with the basic document howsoever, i.e., approve it, reject it or demand that it be changed. The purpose of the basic document is merely to make the legal system of a religious community and the principles of its organization available to state bodies and to the general public, i.e., to third persons who come into contact with the religious community. Not only does each religious community present its basic document in the registration proceedings, but it is also entitled to alter and amend this document on its own initiative at any time after the registration.

51. *See* Act No. 3/2002 Sb., s. 10.

Chapter 3. Fundamental Rights and Religious Communities

124. The code of fundamental rights in the Czech Republic is the Charter of Fundamental Rights and Freedoms of 9 January 1991, promulgated as a schedule to constitutional Act No. 23/1991 Sb., which came into effect in the territory of the Czech lands on 4 February 1991. On the day of the dissolution of Czechoslovakia into two independent states – the Czech Republic and the Slovak Republic, which came about on 1 January 1993 – the new Constitution of the Czech Republic (Constitutional Act No. 1/1993 Sb.) came into force. Under Articles 3 and 112, the aforementioned Charter of Fundamental Rights and Freedoms forms a part of the constitutional order of the Czech Republic; it is deemed as the second part of the Constitution and was published again in the Collection of Laws of the Czech Republic under No. 2/1993 Sb. The catalogue of fundamental rights contained in the Charter is based on similar provisions found in international treaties binding in the Czech Republic on the date of its publication. These were the following international treaties: the International Covenant on Civil and Political Rights (1966) and the International Covenant on Economic, Social and Cultural Rights (1966). When drafting the Charter of Fundamental Rights and Freedoms, the legislature was also inspired by international catalogues of human rights contained in the Universal Declaration of Human Rights adopted by the United Nations on 10 December 1948, and in the European Convention for the Protection of Human Rights and Fundamental Freedoms (ECHR) of 4 November 1950, which has been binding in the Czech Republic since 18 March 1992. The Charter 'declares that it stems from the natural rights philosophy and its historical and current sources. The concept of the *natural rights* of a human was the most significant source when creating the Charter'.[52]

125. The Charter of Fundamental Rights and Freedoms consists of the preamble and six chapters. Chapter 1 (Articles 1–4), General Provisions, is followed by Chapter 2 (Articles 5–23) called Human Rights and Fundamental Freedoms, which is divided into two divisions: Fundamental Human Rights and Freedoms (Articles 5–16) and Political Rights (Articles 17–23). Chapter 3 (Articles 24–25) is designated The Rights of National and Ethnic Minorities; Chapter 4 (Articles 26–35) is titled Economic, Social and Cultural Rights; Chapter 5 (Articles 36–40) is The Right to Judicial and Other Legal Protection; Chapter 6 (Articles 41–44) again contains General Provisions.

126. Articles 5–16 comprise the following fundamental human rights: the right of everyone to possess rights; the right to life; the inviolability of a person and his privacy; personal rights (the right to dignity, personal honour, good reputation and the right to protection of name); the right to protection of private and family life; protection of privacy of correspondence; the right to personal liberty; the right to freedom of movement and residence; the right to the inviolability of a dwelling; a ban on forced labour or service; the right to own property; and freedom of thought, conscience, religion, scientific research and artistic expression. Political rights (Articles 17–23) embody: the freedom of expression and the right to information; the right of petition; the right to assembly; the right to associate; and the right of defence.

52. Václav Pavlíček et al.*Ústavní právo a státověda, II. díl, Ústavní právo České republiky [Constitutional Law and Political Science, Volume II, Constitutional Law of the Czech Republic]*463(Leges, 2011).

127. As for the basic rights of individuals and of religious communities to freely manifest their religion, they are expressly referred to in Articles 3, 15 and 16 of the Charter of Fundamental Rights and Freedoms. Apart from the provisions contained therein, there are also provisions of Articles 17, 19 and 20, which concern the same rights to a considerable extent. All those provisions have already been dealt with in detail in Part I, Chapter 1.

Chapter 4. Contractual Religious Freedom

§1. Basic Principles and Terminology

128. The fall of the communist regime during November and December 1989 was followed by the development of a democratic legal order in both parts of Czechoslovakia: in the Czech Republic and the Slovak Republic. A model which combines contractual regulation with state laws has prevailed.[53]The foundation of the system is the principle of the non-confessional state. The state does not identify itself with any religion or ideology (inclusive of atheism), but observes the principal of parity with regard to all religious communities. The state cooperates with religious communities in matters of common interest. The Czech Republic is defined as a non-confessional or secular state of a cooperative nature.

129. The Czech legal system does not encompass any express provisions requiring that the relationship between religious communities be regulated by agreements. That, however, does not mean that the contractual regulation is not allowed. It is excluded neither by the constitution nor by legislation of the Czech Republic, and it is used in practice as an important and very practical complement to the statutory regulation.

130. The first possibility relied on is a concordat and concordat agreements entered into by and between the Apostolic See and the Czech Republic. They are international agreements without distinguishing whether there is one undivided agreement, or one main agreement and other incidental agreements, or a system of several agreements. The concordat agreements have a long tradition in central Europe (Germany, Austria and all countries bordering the two in the east). After 1990, such agreements with the Apostolic See have been concluded not only by new lands of Germany (the former German Democratic Republic) but also by almost all post-communist countries in east-central Europe.[54]The Czech State has also, in the course of history, entered into several concordat agreements, attempting to conclude the last one in 2002. Guarantees of religious freedoms granted to the Catholic Church by the concordat agreement implicitly bring about the same protection of other religious communities. Therefore, other religious communities in the Czech Republic do not raise any objections to the concluding of the concordat agreements. In the Czech legal order, concluding a concordat agreement does not impede the parity of religious societies, it rather reinforces it.

131. The other possibility of how to supplement the effective legal order with provisions flowing from negotiations with representatives of religious communities is the concluding of domestic agreements between state authorities and individual

53. *See* Jiří Tretera, *Concordatarian Agreements and Public Agreements in the Czech State Ecclesiastical Law*, in *Religion and Law in Dialogue: Covenantal and Non-covenantal Cooperation Between State and Religion in Europe*33 (ed., Richard Puza & Norman Doe 2006).

54. *See* Damián Němec, *Concordat Agreements Between the Holy See and the Post-Communist Countries 1990–2010*87–92(Peeters 2012).

religious communities, which has been effectuated by numerous agreements focusing on particular areas of the activity of religious communities in the public sphere. Parties to agreements entered into so far have been a public authority of the Czech Republic on one side, and the Ecumenical Council of Churches in the Czech Republic (the union of churches acting in the name of eleven religious communities that are regular members thereof)[55]and the Czech Bishops' Conference (the local representative of the Catholic Church comprising bishops working in all dioceses of Roman Catholic and Greek Catholic churches in the Czech Republic)[56]on the other side. The Ecumenical Council of Churches and the Czech Bishops' Conference are, therefore, a joint party to all agreements.

§2. The Tradition of Church–State Agreements in the Czech Lands

132. In Czech history, church–state relations were regulated by unilateral legislative acts of the state, complemented from time to time by a concordat. The first concordat between the Czech Kingdom and the Holy See was concluded in 1221/1222 (the so-called negotiations of Schatzenberg). During the Hussite time, the Basel Compact was concluded (1434). At the beginning of the Counter-Reformation, a concordat between Ferdinand II, the Czech King and Roman Emperor, and the Holy See was concluded (1630); it was later cancelled by Joseph II, the Czech King and Roman Emperor (1782). Between 1855 and 1870, the Austrian Imperial Concordat was in effect.

133. The state–church relations in the new Czechoslovak Republic were regulated exclusively by state legislation. Some legal provisions were adopted from Austria–Hungary, while others were newly created by the new democratic state. However, the above-mentioned relations were regulated also by a concordat agreement at the intergovernmental level known as the *Modus Vivendi.*

134. The *Modus Vivendi*, concluded between the Czechoslovak Government and the Apostolic See in 1927/1928, concerned the appointment of diocesan bishops in the territory of Czechoslovakia. The Apostolic See committed itself to enquire, before the appointment of a diocesan bishop, whether the Government of the Republic had any objections to the candidate. The bishops pledged to a representative of the state that they would not act against the unity and integrity of the state. The Apostolic See also committed itself to adjust Church districts administered by bishops to the state borders and undertook that no religious house (either a monastery or a convent) would be subordinated to a major religious superior outside the territory of the state.

55. The Ecumenical Council of Churches in the Czech Republic represents eleven member churches: Evangelical Church of Czech Brethren, Silesian Evangelical Church A. C., Church of Brethren, Unity of Brethren (Moravian Church), Evangelical Church A. C. in CR, Unity of Baptists, Evangelical Methodist Church, Czechoslovak Hussite Church, Old Catholic Church, Orthodox Church in the Czech Lands, Apostolic Church (Pentecostal Church).
56. The Czech Bishops' Conference represents eight RomanCatholic dioceses (or two archdioceses and six dioceses), and one GreekCatholic exarchate.

135. The *Modus Vivendi* had not been formally cancelled after the coup of February 1948, but 'soon after February 1948 it was clear that the state power would not take account of it'.[57] In late December 1989, during the first visit of representatives of the first post-communist democratic government of Czechoslovakia to the Vatican City following the Velvet Revolution, both parties declared the *Modus Vivendi* void because of the fundamental change in circumstances. *Clausula rebus sic stantibus*, a principle of international law, was applied. On the basis of that declaration, the Czechoslovak Parliament passed a law which put an end to state interference with the appointment of any church ministers, including bishops.[58] Since then, Catholic diocesan bishops have been appointed by the Apostolic See without prior consultation with state authorities. The creation of dioceses does not require state consent either. New Roman Catholic dioceses in Pilsen (1993) and Ostrava–Opava (1996), and a Greek Catholic exarchate in the Czech Republic (1996), were established by the Pope without prior negotiations with the state.

§3. Negotiations on New Concordat Agreement

136. In April 1990, Pope John Paul II visited Czechoslovakia for the first time, following an invitation from the President of the Republic. Diplomatic relations between Czechoslovakia and the Apostolic See were restored in June 1990.[59] While in the period 1920–1939, diplomatic relations were maintained at the level of the nunciature and legacy, and in the period 1945–1950 at the level of the internunciature[60] and legacy, in June 1990 they were re-established at the highest level again: a nunciature and an embassy.

137. The idea for an international agreement with the Apostolic See emerged after the third visit of Pope John Paul II to the Czech Republic in 1997. The social–democratic government appointed in 1998 decided to carry out the idea.

138. On 2 November 1999, the ambassador of the Czech Republic to the Apostolic See stressed at the meeting of a specialist committee at the Ministry of Culture that the basic role of the agreement – and of further possible agreements – is specially to confirm, deepen and guarantee at the international level the rights already existent in the domestic legal order. The President of the Republic, Mr Václav Havel, expressed the wish to conclude the agreement during his visit to the Holy Father at Christmas 1999, on the occasion of the delivery of a Christmas tree to the Vatican City

57. Damián Němec, *Concordat Agreements Between the Holy See and the Post-Communist Countries 1990–2010*, 98–99 (Peeters 2012).
58. Act No. 16/1990 Sb., 23 Jan. 1990.
59. *See* Jiří Rajmund Tretera, *The Czech Bishops' Conference and the Process of Democratisation in the Czech Republic*, in *Chiesa cattolica ed Europa centro-orientale* 68 (ed., Antonio G. Chizzoniti, Vita e Pensiero 2004).
60. This change was initiated in 1945 by Soviet diplomacy, which had sternly insisted that the ambassador of the Soviet Union in Prague be given the position of a doyen of diplomatic corps, as the recognition of the role of the Soviet Union as the 'Liberator' of Czechoslovakia. According to international custom, the position of the doyen was reserved for the Apostolic nuncio. Therefore, his title had to be changed to internuntio.

as a gift from the Czech Republic. As of April 2000, a commission of representatives of both parties worked on a draft of the agreement – it was more than a framework agreement, although the possibility of additional agreements was not excluded. Preparatory work was successfully completed on 28 May 2002 in the presence of Mons. Erwin Josef Ender, the new nuncio in Prague. The agreement was signed by the Minister of Foreign Affairs and the nuncio on 25 July 2002. However, on 21 May 2003, the Chamber of Deputies of the Parliament did not approve the agreement by a majority of 110 votes out of 200 representatives (177 being present at the vote).[61]

139. It seems the reasons for this decision were not related to the content of the agreement. Sometime before, a conflict concerning the new Act on churches and religious societies (Act No. 3/2002 Sb.) had arisen between the Chamber of Deputies on the one hand and the Senate and the President on the other. In the end, the Act on churches and religious societies was passed by a majority of 111 votes of the representatives (in December 2001). However, in November 2002, the Act was amended by the Constitutional Court. It comes as no surprise that the Chamber of Deputies did not incline to approve the agreement in May 2003.

140. The Chamber of Deputies can vote on the agreement again in the future and approve it when the conditions for this are more favourable. Another solution is also possible: to prepare a new concordat agreement. For the time being, it is to be emphasized that the agreement is not ratified, and therefore, it is not a part of the Czech legal order, but neither was it rescinded. No legislation may be adopted which would be contrary to the agreement.

§4. Contents of the Concordat Agreement from 2002

141. The most important articles of the agreement can be summarized as follows:

(1) The Czech Republic recognizes the legal personality of the Roman Catholic Church and Greek Catholic Church, both of them being a part of the Catholic Church (Article 3 paragraph 1). The Apostolic See shall ensure that the borders of Roman Catholic dioceses and Apostolic administrative territories, as well as Greek Catholic eparchies and exarchates, coincide with the borders of the state (Article 3 paragraph 2);

(2) The Apostolic See takes into account that the Czech Republic is, in accordance with its constitutional order, a non-denominational state, and it is not linked to any religion (Article 5 paragraph 1);

(3) The Czech Republic guarantees to the Catholic Church the right to freely realize its mission. It guarantees to the Catholic Church the right to administer its own affairs, especially to appoint, change or dismiss its organs and its internal structures independently and according to its own needs, and to nominate, appoint and dismiss its ministers and other persons providing pastoral service (Article 6);

61. *See* Jiří Rajmund Tretera, *Concordatarian Agreements and Public Agreements in the Czech State Ecclesiastical Law*, in *Religion and Law in Dialogue: Covenantal and Non-covenantal Cooperation Between State and Religion in Europe* 36–37 (ed., Richard Puza & Norman Doe, 2006).

(4) No one may be forced to perform military service as far as it is contrary to his or her conscience or religious conviction (Article 7);
(5) The Catholic form of marriage has the same consequences as the civil form (Article 9);
(6) Legal persons, especially in the areas of education, healthcare, social care and charity, established under the regulations of the Catholic Church (canon law) have legal personality under Czech law provided the conditions stipulated by Czech law have been fulfilled (Article 10 paragraph 1);
(7) Catholic charities are administered in accordance with their own bylaws and have the right to be financed from the state budget, as is the case with all establishments of analogous character (Article 13 paragraph 2).

142. The Agreement regulates the right to establish church schools (Article 10 paragraph 2, Article 11 paragraph 1), the right to religious education and its control, including *missio canonica* (Article 11 paragraphs 5–6) in more detail. University bodies may approve constitutions of Catholic theological schools only with the prior consent of the Church authority (Article 11 paragraph 4).[62]The right to have academic degrees in religious sciences from public and church theological schools abroad is guaranteed (Article 11 paragraph 3).

143. The right to pastoral service in prisons and in the army is declared by referring to the agreement between the Czech Bishops' Conference and a competent state authority (Articles 15 and 16).

144. As far as a definitive solution of property issues is concerned, Article 17 contains the commitment of the Czech Republic as soon as possible to reach a settlement in the matter. A possible new model of financing may lessen economical anxieties of the Catholic Church in the meantime.[63]

145. The Czech Bishops' Conference is authorized to negotiate on the affairs affecting the entire Catholic Church in the Czech Republic, especially as to the provision of new or additional solutions; negotiations between the parties to the agreement are not affected thereby (Article 18 paragraph 1). These affairs can be settled by resolutions between the parties to the agreement or between competent state authorities and the Czech Bishops' Conference with the consent of the Apostolic See (Article 18 paragraph 2).

62. This is guaranteed by Act No. 111/1998 Sb., on Universities.
63. These requirements have been fulfilled by Act No. 428/2012 Sb., on Property Settlement with Churches and Religious Societies. The Act is not merely a reaction to the wording of said concordat agreement, but primarily to the principle of the protection of proprietary rights expressed in the Charter of Fundamental Rights and Freedoms. Last but not least, it reacts to the finding of the Constitutional Court of 2 Feb. 2005 (file No. II ÚS 528/02) and to other findings thereof, which stipulated the obligation of the legislature to enact a restitution Act, meeting thereby, legitimate expectations of religious communities regarding their historical properties.

§5. Domestic Church–State Agreements

146. Domestic agreements with religious entities have been used since 1994. Making use of this method, the legal regulation has developed well since then. In the Czech Republic, there is a detailed regulation of the activities of religious communities in the following public institutions: prisons, the army, police forces, fire rescue services, public health and social establishments, and Czech Radio.

I. Prisons

147. The activity of religious communities in prison services, which safeguards the exercising of the religious freedom of inmates as well as aids their social rehabilitation, has a long tradition in the Czech lands, interrupted only during the period of communist rule. Despite this, religious communities had a good position for a swift restoration of this activity as early as 1990. The reason is obvious: both clerical and lay members of religious communities had vast personal experience of prison services from the time of the totalitarian regime. After all, many of them were themselves held prisoner even in the 1980s! Among the first prison chaplains in the Czech Republic were priests and preachers who had served their imprisonment sentences as prisoners of conscience at the very places where they began to provide care after the Revolution and were, therefore, well acquainted with the local conditions. They were familiar with the mentality and problems of persons convicted of various crimes as well as with most of the prison personnel.

148. The recovery of the activity of religious communities in prison services was enabled by Act No. 179/1990 Sb., which amended the then effective Act No. 59/1965 Sb., on the Execution of Punishment of Imprisonment. In order to reinforce the status of representatives of religious communities who had been visiting prisons to provide spiritual care to inmates since 1990, and to specify their status and competences, there was the first agreement between state authorities and representatives of religious communities, concluded on 7 January 1994. The parties to the agreement were the Prison Service of the Czech Republic, the Ecumenical Council of Churches in the Czech Republic and the Czech Bishops' Conference. Based on this agreement, the previous inconsistently organized system of care provided by pastors in whose parishes the prisons were located was replaced by an efficient system of caring for inmates provided by representatives of various religious communities.

149. Any person kept in prison has the right to talk to a minister of any religious community according to his own choice; no one shall be forced upon him. Ministers who visit prisons undertake that they will render care to anyone, regardless of denomination, even to members of other than Christian religions and, in particular, also to those who are not members of any religion. Since the beginning, the ministers have been providing their services ecumenically, without any confessional restriction. Those who have, based on the agreement of 1994, chosen to carry out their mission of providing spiritual service in prisons as their vocation have been referred to as prison chaplains, both male and female; they may be accepted as employees of the Prison Service of the Czech Republic upon a recommendation by their religious community, and they make up a board of chaplains, called the Ecumenical Prison Chaplaincy, headed by the Head Chaplain.

150. The Ecumenical Prison Chaplaincy cooperates with a civil registered association called Prison Spiritual Care, which also sends to prisons, upon the consent of the administration thereof, its representatives, who carry out tasks of spiritual care, including interviews with inmates, and who do so without being paid, alongside their regular jobs. Any person assigned to the task by Prison Spiritual Care is obliged to visit a prison facility a minimum of twice per month. Said civil registered association is an association on a voluntary basis of Christians of various denominations. It is an extra-denominational organization of the ecumenical nature, whose associates may be members of religious communities in both degree of registration as well as of religious communities that have not yet been registered.

151. The activity of the Ecumenical Prison Chaplaincy has proven itself since 1994 and has gradually spread to virtually all prisons. In practice, however, the need for a yet clearer legal specification of the status of all bodies working spiritually in prisons was high. Therefore, the original agreement was soon replaced by a new one, concluded by and between the same parties on 28 June 1999. Another agreement, the third in order, was entered into on 18 August 2008, the fourth one was entered into on 21 November 2013.

152. Each of those agreements regulated the cooperation between the Prison Service of the Czech Republic, the administration of prison facilities, and religious communities regarding their spiritual and rehabilitation impact on the accused, the convicted and inmates in detention facilities. A precondition of the activity in prisons is the authorization by a religious community and a clean criminal record. Authorized persons who are employees of the Prison Service of the Czech Republic are referred to as prison chaplains. Currently, the chaplains, members of ten different religious communities, are the employees of the Prison Service of the Czech Republic, and, at the same time, associates of the civil association of Prison Spiritual Care. They operate in twenty-three prisons and remand prisons and their number totals around thirty-five persons. The Head Chaplain is a female at the moment. There are some Catholic female chaplains (they are pastoral assistants). A certain number of other representatives authorized by religious communities work outside the employment relationship and even greater is the number of volunteers assigned by the civil association of Prison Spiritual Care.

II. Military Chaplaincy

153. On the basis of an informal agreement between the representatives of the Catholic Church and the Ministry of Defence, the first two Catholic military chaplains began to serve in the armed forces of the Czech Republic in 1996, participating in the international peace missions IFOR and SFOR, operating in the former Yugoslavia. Their presence and activity was successful. Following this, the agreement on cooperation between the Ministry of Defence of the Czech Republic, the Czech Bishops' Conference and the Ecumenical Council of Churches in the Czech Republic was concluded on 3

June 1998. The agreement was implemented by the Order of the Minister of Defence on the establishment of a pastoral service, which came into force on 22 June 1998.

154. Military chaplains are officers. They are appointed upon the collective nomination of all the religious communities which are parties to the agreement. Internal subordination of military chaplains in the organizational structure of their religious community is not affected. Conditions for the appointment of a military chaplain are prescribed in the above-mentioned agreement between the Ministry of Defence of the Czech Republic, the Ecumenical Council of Churches in the Czech Republic and the Czech Bishops' Conference from 1998. Both these last institutions had bound themselves to evenly replenish the total number of military chaplains so that it reached twenty-five, which happened within the ensuing ten years. According to another agreement, this time between the Czech Bishops' Conference and the Ecumenical Council of Churches in the Czech Republic only, the number of military chaplains should have been annually topped up by two Catholic chaplains and one chaplain from another religious community. The total number of military chaplains under this agreement was composed of two-thirds of chaplains sent out upon the nomination by the Czech Bishops' Conference and one-third upon the nomination by the Ecumenical Council of Churches in the Czech Republic.

155. The group of military chaplains is headed by the Head Chaplain of the Army of the Czech Republic, who is appointed for a period of four years, and whose term is renewable one time by the Minister of Defence of the Czech Republic upon the common nomination by the Ecumenical Council of Churches in the Czech Republic and the Czech Bishops' Conference. This person is subordinated to the Chief of the General Staff. There is one minister in the civilian section of the Ministry of Defence of the Czech Republic, appointed jointly by the Ecumenical Council of Churches in the Czech Republic and the Czech Bishops' Conference, who acts as an external advisor of the Minister of Defence onmatters of military spiritual care. The agreement concluded between said parties stipulates that one of the aforementioned highest positions is filled by the Ecumenical Council of Churches in the Czech Republic, and the other by the Czech Bishops' Conference.The Czech Bishops' Conference deputed the Archbishop of Prague to carry out external control of military chaplains of Catholic denomination in the sense of canon law.

156. The activity of spiritual service abides by the following principles: ecumenicity, time limitation (usually for the period of four years with a possibility of repeating) and being primarily non-missionary. The purpose of the activity of military chaplains is not to spread faith. Spiritual services and talks are provided to soldiers who show an interest therein, regardless of denomination, as well as to those without any denominational affiliation. Military chaplains cooperate with psychologists of the Army of the Czech Republic. They are directly subordinated to commanding officers (usually at the level of a regiment or even a higher military unit). They are assigned to those units whose commanding officers expressly desire so.

157. To qualify for the position of a military chaplain, the following prerequisites must be fulfilled: a university degree (typically in theology), at least two years of active participation in the religious administration of a religious community at the post of a minister, and the willingness to create friendly ecumenical relationships among military chaplains. The express commission to serve as a military chaplain by the person's own religious community and a subsequent authorization by the Czech Bishops' Conference and the Ecumenical Council of Churches in the Czech Republic are required. Last but not least, there are the requirements of reasonable medical fitness, physical preparedness corresponding with standards for joining the Army of the Czech Republic, and a good psychological profile and family background. Military chaplains undergo military training, except for the use of arms. Upon the expiration of time the chaplains have been appointed for, they become civilians and usually return to pastoral service in their religious communities.

158. The experience with the military chaplains service has proven to be very good,and their activity has proven beneficial, not only during rescue work after disasters (e.g., during floods) and military missions of the Czech Army abroad (in the Middle East, Afghanistan) but also during military training, exercises and at military schools, all that even in the fully professional army (as of 2005). Therefore, the Ministry of Defence requested that the above-mentioned agreement be amended, which happened on 26 January 2012, and the number of military chaplains be increased to forty, specifically twenty from the Catholic Church, seven from the Czechoslovak Hussite Church, five from the Evangelical Church of Czech Brethren, two from the Church of Brethren, and one each from the Seventh-Day Adventists Church, Orthodox Church, Silesian Evangelical Church A. C., Unity of the Brethren, Old Catholic Church and the Evangelical Church A. C. As of 2015, the ranks of military chaplains should be joined by representatives of the Evangelical Methodist Church, Apostolic Church and Unity of Brethren Baptists.

III. Police and Fire Rescue Services

159. The first agreement on the participation of religious communities in the provision of post-traumatic intervention care for the members of the Police of the Czech Republic was entered into by and between the Ministry of the Interior of the Czech Republic, the Czech Bishops' Conference and the Ecumenical Council of Churches in the Czech Republic on 7 October 2002. On the grounds of the agreement, selected ministers were assigned to teams helping the police to solve mentally demanding situations (encounters of death, serious traffic accidents, use of a service weapon causing irreversible effects).

160. Ministers also participate in psychosocial intervention teams, in which they act along with psychologists, social workers and workers of non-profit organizations. All members of these teams, including ministers, undergo a special year-long training. Their work is focused on helping victims of disasters, terrorist attacks and individual or mass accidents.

161. An agreement on cooperation between the Director General of Fire Rescue Services (which is subordinated to the Ministry of the Interior), the Czech Bishops' Conference and the Ecumenical Council of Churches in the Czech Republic was concluded at the beginning of 2003. It was a reaction to the disastrous floods in Bohemia in 2002. Participating religious communities undertook that should similar crisis situations occur, they would contribute both spiritually and materially to helping the victims. The task of religious communities is to provide workers of charities and diaconias, to organize volunteers and to assure the distribution of material help. Fire Rescue Services undertook to secure conditions for the activity of ministers and workers of charities and diaconias in crisis committees, as well as to ensure the possibility of entering into similar agreements with fire brigades on a regional level.

162. Also in the case of fire rescue services there is a system of post-traumatic intervention care. Its first grounds were the guidance notes issued by the director of Fire Rescue Services and a deputy of the Minister of the Interior on8 September 2003, which counts on the participation of ministers sent out jointly by the Czech Bishops' Conference and the Ecumenical Council of Churches in the Czech Republic.

163. Further, more detailed regulation was brought about by a complex agreement of 6 October 2011, entered into by and between the Ministry of the Interior of the Czech Republic, the Ecumenical Council of Churches and the Czech Bishops' Conference, on the participation of persons providing spiritual service in the system of post-traumatic intervention care. Based on this agreement, intervention care is rendered by ministers of participating religious communities to policemen, firemen, employees of the Police, and the Ministry of the Interior, their family members and their next of kin. Care is also provided to members of the general public who have become victims of emergencies or crimes. Said services are provided free of charge; ministers and their assistants, who have been commissioned thereto by their religious communities, are, according to the agreement, entitled to transport to the place of the rendition of intervention care.

IV. Public Health

164. The absence of legal regulation and an agreement providing for the access of representatives of religious communities to hospitals, long-stay hospitals and residential care homes, and guaranteeing the exercising of the religious freedom of patients in said facilities, have been seen as a shortcoming for a long time. The need for the regulation is greater in cases where the ability of the patient to move and his contact with the outside world is limited (accident, operation, placement into an intensive care unit), or the contact of the patient with the outside world is hindered by his immobility or advanced age, or by necessary isolation (placement into the isolation ward, psychiatric ward, etc.).

165. We have seen positive changes in said area as well. On 20 November 2006, the agreement on Spiritual Care in Health Service was concluded between the Czech Bishops' Conference and the Ecumenical Council of Churches in the Czech Republic; an amendment thereto was executed on 12 December 2011. The two documents regulate the sending of hospital chaplains and volunteers to healthcare facilities in order to do good to the suffering, regardless of their denomination.

166. The hospital chaplains and volunteers are sent out to healthcare facilities based on a written agreement between a religious community practising on the site where the facility is located and the facility itself. The sending religious community may, in relation to the facility, represent multiple religious communities who have agreed thereon.

167. A hospital chaplain is a person who provides spiritual care in a healthcare facility as a member of a multidisciplinary team on the grounds of the authorization (a letter of appointment) granted by their religious community and an agreement with the facility. In the case of the Catholic Church, the authorization is given by a diocesan bishop or exarch. In the case of religious communities who are the members of the Ecumenical Council of Churches in the Czech Republic, the authorization is obtained from the respective body determined by the internal regulation of the community; it is either the highest representative of the church or a representative of its higher administrative unit.

168. A volunteer in the field of spiritual care is a person who, in their free time and under the guidance of a hospital chaplain, participates in spiritual care in a healthcare facility and is authorized thereto by their own religious community.

169. The appointment of hospital chaplains, and modifications and termination thereof, isnotified by the respective religious communities to competent coordinating bodies of the Czech Bishops' Conference and the Ecumenical Council of Churches in the Czech Republic, as well as to the representatives of all affected religious communities on the given site.

170. Besides the authorization by their own religious community, a hospital chaplain must meet the following qualification prerequisites: a master's in theology, at least three years of practice in general pastoral care, and the completion of a specialized course in hospital chaplaincy (or a corresponding qualification). A hospital chaplain is obliged to become familiar with the general principles of pastoral care and the basics of the organization of the Catholic Church and other individual churches that are members of the Ecumenical Council of Churches in the Czech Republic and to have knowledge of all religious communities operating in the Czech Republic, of bioethics, of the organization of healthcare, etc. The qualification prerequisites for the work of a volunteer are somewhat lower.

171. Provisions of the Agreement of the Spiritual Care in Healthcare are used analogously for residential care homes and other similar facilities. The Agreement applies to the Catholic Church and communities associated in the Ecumenical Council of Churches in the Czech Republic. Religious communities have undertaken that when deciding on the choice of candidates for hospital chaplaincy, they will look to the personal qualities of the candidate, namely to ecumenical openness (cooperation with ministers of other religious communities) and to the ability to communicate.

172. In order to reinforce the activity of religious communities in the field of spiritual care in healthcare, the Association of Hospital Chaplains was set up in 2011, a civil association, on the board of which there are mainly representatives of Protestant Churches. Its objective is the support of education, the raising of public awareness and safeguarding a quality, professional spiritual and pastoral care for the ill, their next of kin, medical personnel and chaplains. In 2012, the Catholic Association of Hospital Chaplains, which unites all Catholic hospital chaplains, was established for the same purpose.

173. The Czech legal order contains the regulation of spiritual care in healthcare in Act No. 372/2011 Sb., on Healthcare Services and Conditions for providing them. The Act stipulates that an inpatient has the right to spiritual care provided by any registered religious community. A patient shall not be denied the visit of a minister in the case that their life is at risk or their health may be seriously damaged. No agreement between the state, or other public bodies, and religious communities that would provide detailed regulation of the activity of hospital chaplains in healthcare facilities has yet been concluded.

V. Radio and Television

174. The agreement on cooperation between Czech Radio (the public radio station), the Czech Bishops' Conference, and the Ecumenical Council of Churches in the Czech Republic was concluded on 19 December 1995, and a new agreement was concluded on 29 June 1999. They are agreements between public corporations and religious communities.

175. Czech public television and representatives of the Catholic and Protestant Churches created a special board for religious broadcasting. It operates not only without an agreement with religious communities but also without any controversy.

Part IV. International, Transnational, Regional Effects on Religious Communities

Chapter 1. International Law Effects on Religious Communities

176. 'Promulgated international treaties, the ratification of which has been approved by the Parliament and which are binding in the Czech Republic, shall constitute a part of the legal order; should an international treaty make provisions contrary to a law, the treaty shall prevail.'[64] This implies that international treaties come second in the hierarchy of rules of law of the Czech Republic, directly after constitutional Acts.

177. The Czech Republic has signed and ratified all relevant international treaties concerning freedom of religion. High on the list of international treaties, which are binding in the Czech Republic, are the following:

- The International Covenant on Civil and Political Rights (1966), since 23 March 1976;
- The International Covenant on Economic, Social and Cultural Rights (1966), since 23 March 1976;
- The Convention on the Rights of the Child (1989), since 6 February 1991;
- The Convention Relating to the Status of Refugees (1951), since 24 February 1992;
- The European Convention for the Protection of Human Rights and Fundamental Freedoms (1950), since 18 March 1992.

178. The process of implementation of human rights, including freedom of religion, into the Czech legal order, was influenced not only by the above-mentioned international treaties, but also by main international declarations, chiefly by:

- The Universal Declaration of Human Rights adopted by the United Nations on 10 December 1948; and
- The Declaration on the Elimination of All Forms of and of Discrimination Based on Religion or Belief adopted by the United Nations on 25 November 1981.

64. Constitutional Act No. 1/1993 Sb., Constitution of the Czech Republic, Art. 10.

179. As for bilateral international treaties, no such treaties have been concluded, because there is no need for them. The only exceptions are Concordats or Concordat Agreements with the Apostolic See.[65]The last Concordat Agreement between the Czech Republic and the Apostolic See was signed on 25 July 2002, but it has not yet been ratified.[66]

---

65. *See* Damián Němec, *Concordat Agreements Between the Holy See and the Post-Communist Countries 1990–2010* (Peeters 2012).
66. The preceding Agreement between Czechoslovakia and the Apostolic See called *Modus Vivendi* was concluded on 2 Feb. 1928. In late December 1989, both parties to this Agreement declared it void because of the fundamental change in circumstances. It happened during the first visit of the representatives of the first post-communist democratic government of Czechoslovakia to the Vatican City following the Velvet Revolution.

Chapter 2. Transnational Law Effects on Religious Communities

180. On 4 November 1950, the Council of Europe, established in 1949, adopted the ECHR. After the democratic revolution in Czechoslovakia at the end of 1989, nothing hindered the country from acceding to the said integration organization, which protects and promotes the observance of human rights on the European continent. Czechoslovakia was accepted in 1991 and has been bound by the Convention since 18 March 1992, when it came into effect.[67] After the peaceful dissolution of Czechoslovakia at the end of 1992, the Czech Republic remained bound by the Convention, and it was newly accepted into the Council of Europe on 30 June 1993. The ECHR continues to be a key document that influences the legal status of religious communities in the Czech Republic.

181. Article 9 of the ECHR was an inspiration for Article 16 of the *Charter of Fundamental Rights and Freedoms* of 9 January 1991, which was adopted even before the formal ratification of the ECHR by Czechoslovakia.[68]

182. Regarding the European Court of Human Rights in Strasbourg, established by the Council of Europe, there is no doubt that it is of great importance for all Member States:

> Considering the influence of the European Court's case law on the legal regulation of the freedom of religion or on the status of religious communities in the Czech Republic, there are two possible types of such influence: direct influence, where the European Court declares a violation of the Convention in proceedings against the Czech Republic, thereby having an effect on either the decision-making practice of national courts or immediately on the wording of the legislation, or indirect influence, where courts or the legislature are familiar with the European Court's case law and they carry out their activity in accordance therewith. In relation to the Czech Republic, the European Court has ruled on several complaints regarding interference with the right to religious freedom. It has found all complaints inadmissible. The most important may be deemed the decision in the case Juraj Lajda et al. v. the Czech Republic of 3 March 2009, file no. 20984/05, which regarded the legal regulation of the registration of churches and religious societies. Another key decision was the one in the case Dudová and Duda v. the Czech Republic of 30 January 2001, file no. 40224/98; the complainants mainly claimed a breach of Art. 6, sec. 1 of the Convention (the right to fair trial);

67. *See* Notice of the Federal Ministry of Foreign Affairs of the Czech and Slovak Federative Republic No. 209/1992 Sb.
68. *See* Jiří Rajmund Tretera, Záboj Horák, *The Application of the Freedom of Religion Principles of the European Convention on Human Rights in the Czech Republic*, in *Religious Freedom in the European Union*99 (ed., Achilles Emilianides,Peeters 2011).

materially, however, the subject of the dispute was the extent of the autonomy of religious communities when appointing and dismissing ministers.[69]

183. On 1 May 2004, the Czech Republic became a member of EU. EU legislation is traditionally concerned with economic matters, and the relationship between a state and religious communities is reserved for legal regulation by Member States. However, it shall not go unnoticed that legal rules of EU also emphasize the right to religious freedom and reinforce the provisions of international conventions that have been so far concluded and that are binding in the Czech Republic and are reflected in its legislation and in the decision-making practice of courts. One example of the direct influence of EU law on Czech law is the Czech Anti-discrimination Act (Act No. 198/2009 Sb.)[70]

69. Jakub Kříž, *Vliv judikatury Evropského soudu pro lidská práva na náboženskou svobodu v České republice* [Influence of Case Law of the European Court of Human Rights on Religious Freedom in the Czech Republic]37*Jurisprudence* 7–8 (2012).

70. *See* Jiří Rajmund Tretera, Záboj Horák, Czech Republic, in *Religion and Discrimination Law in the European Union*89 (ed., Mark Hill QC,Institute for European Constitutional Law, University of Trier 2012).

Chapter 3. Regional Law Effects on Religious Communities

184. The Czech Republic is a unitary state. It is not subdivided into lower units that have their own legislative power. Bodies of local self-government (fourteen regions and several thousand municipalities) have the authority to issue both ordinances in their separate power and regulations of regional and municipal councils in their delegated power. Bodies of local self-government issue both types of local legal rules on the basis of the delegation of authority by a general Act and within its limits (*secundum et intra legem*).[71]Regions and municipalities, as well as the state, are barred by law from conducting either religious or anti-religious activities.[72]However, they are allowed to cooperate with religious communities when fulfilling cultural, conservation, archival, museum, healthcare, social, school, and other educational programmes, as well as on the preservation of nature and the environment.

71. *See* Aleš Gerloch, *Teorie práva [Theory of Law]*84–85(4th ednAleš Čeněk 2007).
72. *See* Act No. 3/2002 Sb., s. 4, subsec. 2.

Part V. Religion and Politics

Chapter 1. Religious Influence in Politics

185. Religious influence in politics in the Czech Republic is exercised mainly at a theoretical level. When carrying out their activity, representatives of politics and of the legislature, on their own initiative, take account of theological and philosophical inferences of religious thinkers. They give effect to documents created by religious communities, particularly by those that are notably represented in Czech society. The elemental Czech textbook of constitutional law says that:

> The standard wording of the Charter was also influenced by the political and social philosophy of Catholicism, the influence of which won out, for example, in a debate on the protection of a yet unborn child. … The influence of Christian, and in particular Catholic, documents is emphasised not only because of the numerousness of members of this religion in the Czech Republic, but also for the real influence of these ideas at that time, which was also strengthened due to the fact that it was not interconnected with the former political power.[73]

186. As for political parties, religious influence comes expressly into play, at a general Christian level, in the Christian and Democratic Union – the Czechoslovak People's Party. The party is not connected with any particular religion. Various religious communities exercise their influence therein through individuals who are their members. Sometimes, there are groups in certain other political parties formed by their faithful members, usually designated as a Christian platform, which inform other members of the respective party of social opinions of religious communities.

187. Integrating organizations which publicly express the opinions of religious communities on political and public issues are the Czech Bishops' Conference, the Ecumenical Council of Churches in the Czech Republic and the Federation of Jewish Communities in the Czech Republic. Although they express their opinions independent of one another in certain cases, they frequently act jointly. To illustrate, in August 2012, chairpersons of the said three organizations issued a statement 'On the current situation regarding the Act on partial property settlement with churches and religious societies', by which they reacted to an aggressive anti-religious campaign in the media and on billboards.

73. Václav Pavlíček et al.*Ústavní právo a státověda, II. díl, Ústavní právo České republiky [Constitutional Law and Politics, Vol. II, Constitutional Law of the Czech Republic]*467 (Leges 2011).

188. Individual religious communities, or rather their chief bodies, also release their statements on political and public issues in the Czech Republic and abroad. A great deal of activity in this respect is performed by the Synodal Council of the Evangelical Church of Czech Brethren.

189. A completely unique organization is thesociety of evangelical Christians called Constance Unity,[74]which was established in 1903 with the aim to 'create a platform for Evangelical churches to carry out their public enlightenment activity in the nation outside of existing churches'.[75]It has been issuing its own weekly magazine called Constance Sparks (Kostnické jiskry), nowadays called Evangelical Weekly Magazine Constance Sparks. The Unity is composed of individuals who join of their own initiative and by no means on the authorization by their own religious communities. It explains common attitudes of Czech Protestants to the public; however, it does not exercise political influence on religious communities.

74. The name is connected with the German city of Constance upon Bodensee, where Master John Hus, a Czech thinker and reformer, was burnt at the stake on 6 Jul. 1415, and his friend Master Jerome of Prague was burnt at the stake on 30 May 1416.

75. Pavel Filipi et al.*Malá encyklopedie evangelických církví [Small Encyclopaedia of Evangelical Churches]*88 (Libri 2008).

Chapter 2. Political Influence in Religion

190. Owing to the constitutionally guaranteed autonomy of religious communities in the Czech Republic, neither a state authority nor a self-governing body is allowed to interfere in either the internal issues or the teachings of any religious community. Neither political parties nor civil associations do so. Based on the case law and practice of the Constitutional Court so far, it can be inferred that such actions may be qualified as inconsistent with the principle of good morals. Having adverse experience from the time of the Nazi and communist totalitarian regimes, religious communities do not allow any such interferences from the outside. In the Czech Republic there aren't any non-religious societies, associations or leagues of religious citizens, be them Christian, Jewish, Islamic or the like, which would exercise external political influence on religious communities.

Chapter 3. Interaction Between Religion and the State on a Political and Legal Level

191. Neither direct interference by the state in the internal matters of religious communities nor political influence by state bodies on religious communities is allowed in the Czech Republic. Under the effective Act No. 3/2002 Sb., on Churches and Religious Societies, religious communities are legally entitled, upon their own motion, to have the religious community registered by virtue of an administrative proceeding carried out by state bodies, to have the special rights of a religious community registered, as well as to have a union of religious communities registered. Religious communities are legally entitled to have legal persons deriving from the religious community recorded. Said administrative proceedings are a significant manifestation of the interaction between a religious community and the state. However, the public bodies do not have a right to express their wishes as to how the religious communities should phrase their claims in these cases either. Should a religious community word its claims so that they contravene either an internationally recognized system of human rights or the legal rules of the Czech state, the claims will be rejected by a public authority.

192. Although, such a possibility is not prohibited by law, religious communities have no legal right to demand that public bodies enter into agreements with them regarding cooperation in matters of common interest. Since 1994, public bodies have been concluding, upon their own initiative, domestic agreements with religious communities regarding the provision of special spiritual care in public institutions, providedthat individual religious communities show interest in such activity. Such cooperation is in line with the principle of a religiously neutral state of a cooperative nature, which the Czech Republic is.

193. Another example of such interactions are negotiations in 2010–2011, upon the initiative of the government as the sponsor of bills, that have been led with representatives of seventeen religious communities that were, after the coup in February 1948, dispossessed of property securing their activity. The negotiations concerned the preparation of a bill regarding the means of property settlement between the state and said religious communities and were initiated by the government at the instigation by the Constitutional Court, which had declared in several findings a duty of the legislature to adopt a restitution Act, meeting thereby legitimate expectations of religious communities in relation to their historical property. Namely, it was the finding of the Constitutional Court of 2 February 2005, file No. II. ÚS 528/02. Crucial was then the influence of the finding of the Constitutional Court of 1 July 2010, file No. Pl. ÚS 9/07, which states that a long-term failure to act by the Parliament of the Czech Republic, consisting in non-adoption of a special legal regulation on the settlement of historical property belonging to religious communities, is unconstitutional and infringes on the Constitution of the Czech Republic, the Charter, of Fundamental Rights and Freedoms and the Additional Protocol to the ECHR.

194. Representatives of the government and the seventeen religious communities reached an agreement on partial property settlement between the state and religious communities on 25 August 2011.[76]The outcomes of the negotiations were incorporated into the bill that was finally passed into law by the Parliament of the Czech Republic on 8 November 2012 as Act No. 428/2012 Sb., on Property Settlement with Churches and Religious Societies. Said Act also repealed at that time the effective Act No. 218/1949 Sb., on the Economic Security of Churches and Religious Societies provided by the State.[77]

76. Jiří Rajmund Tretera, Záboj Horák, *The Mutual Roles of Religion and State in Czech Republic*, in *The Mutual Roles of Religion and State in Europe*41(ed., Balázs Schanda,Institute for European Constitutional Law, University of Trier 2013).

77. For more details *see* Part VIII.,Church Financing.

Part VI. Labour Law Within Religious Communities

Chapter 1. Scope of Application of Labour Law

195. Under Czech labour law, employees enjoy numerous rights in connection with the commencement, course and termination of employment. The relationship between an employer and an employee is regulated by an employment contract, the essentials of which are prescribed by the rules of the labour law of the Czech Republic, contained primarily in a comprehensive code, which is the Labour Code. The Labour Code, which is currently in effect, was promulgated as Act No. 262/2006 Sb. Disputes between an employer and an employee arising out of the employment established by a contract shall be resolved by a court upon a motion filed by one of the parties.

196. The Labour Code applies fully to only a part of the employees of religious communities, namely to those who work for those communities and their branches as parties to a contractually established employment of a non-pastoral nature. The status of persons who have been taken on by religious communities in accordance with their own internal regulations as their ministers or lay pastoral workers differs. Their legal relationship with a religious community is not deemed an employment relationship, but rather a service relationship. It is regulated by the internal rules of the religious community based on a constitutional principle of the autonomy of religious communities.

Chapter 2. Religious Ministers and Labour Law

197. The service relationship of ministers and other pastoral workers within a religious community has been dealt with in more detail by the Constitutional Court, which has adjudicated on said issue several times.

198. The first one is a decision of the Constitutional Court of 26 March 1997, file No. I ÚS 211/96, which rejected the jurisdiction of secular courts in disputes concerning the termination of a service relationship involving members of the clergy and other pastoral employees of religious communities. The process had been initiated by two former ministers of the Czechoslovak Hussite Church – the married couple Z. Duda and E. Dudová – who were unsatisfied with always the same judgments of Czech general courts. According to the opinion of the Constitutional Court, the persons carrying out pastoral service Act on behalf of religious communities shall follow their internal rules. Only religious communities can judge the abilities of these persons for pastoral service and decide on their appointment or dismissal. As a result, state courts do not decide on the appointment of pastoral workers by religious communities, because in such a case they would unduly interfere with the religious communities' internal autonomy and their right to independent decision-making. As for salaries, or rather other civil claims of ministers, state courts are competent, according to Article 7 of the Code of Civil Procedure,[78]to decide on issues of labour law, where the private character of a religious community comes to the fore as a legal entity. In these civil cases, a judicial proceeding does not interfere with the internal autonomy of religious communities and their decision-making power.

199. On 30 January 2001, the European Court of Human Rights decided in the case of *Duda & Dudová v. the Czech Republic* and upheld the argumentation of the Czech Constitutional Court.[79]

200. On 31 August 2000, the Constitutional Court ruled in an analogous case (file No. III. ÚS 136/2000) brought by a former minister of the Unity of Brethren (Moravian Brethren), with the same result.[80]

---

78. Act No. 99/1963 Sb.
79. *Duda and Dudová v. the Czech Republic* (*Dec.*), No. 40224/98, 30 Jan. 2001, ECHR.
80. *See* Jiří Rajmund Tretera, Záboj Horák, *The Application of the Freedom of Religion Principles of the European Convention on Human Rights in the Czech Republic*, in *Religious Freedom in the European Union*101–102 (ed., Achilles Emilianides,Peeters 2011).

Chapter 3. Other Church Employees and Labour Law

201. Other employees of religious communities and their branches are vergers, sacristans, sextons, gravamen, accountants, gardeners, archivists, secretaries, librarians, lawyers, construction supervisors, repairmen, charity workers, economists, professional drivers, cleaners, carers and other social workers who provide care services at institutions or at home, and workers in other professions. There arises, runs and terminates an employment relationship, established by an employment agreement in compliance with the Labour Code, between these employees and individual branches of religious communities, which are legal persons, or as the case may be with the whole religious community, in particular in the case of less numerous religious communities. Courts competent to settle disputes are Czech courts. Not a single case has so far attracted the attention either of the mass media or of professional literature. It is possible that no such case has yet arisen, or that such a case has not attracted significant attention.

Part VII. Religious Communities and Protections of the Individual

Chapter 1. Protection of Privacy

202. Under Czech law, the protection of privacy is regulated by Act No. 101/2000 Sb., on the Protection of Personal Data. This Act was passed in compliance with obligations set by the law of EU[81]and international treaties by which the Czech Republic is bound.[82]The Act guarantees the exercising of everyone's right to protection against the unlawful invasion of privacy, it regulates rights and duties when processing personal data, and it sets the conditions under which personal data is furnished to foreign states.

203. The said Act established the Office for the Protection of Personal Data, located in Prague, which is the central administrative office concerned with the field of the protection of personal data. The law applies to personal data processed by public authorities, bodies of local self-government, other public bodies, as well as by individuals and legal persons. A person intending to process personal data is bound to notify the Office for the Protection of Personal Data of it. The notification duty does not apply to the administration of personal data carried out by religious communities, provided that they process the data regarding their members and the data serve their internal use only.[83]

204. Personal data may be processed by an administrator, thereof, solely with a consent given by the concerned entities. If the consent is not granted, the data may be processed only if it is necessary for carrying out the legitimate activity of religious communities[84](and some other organizations).

81. Directive of the European Parliament and of the Council No. 95/46/EC of 24 Oct. 1995, on the protection of individuals with regard to the processing of personal data and on the free movement of such data.
82. Convention of the Council of Europe No. 108 of 28 Jan. 1981, for the protection of individuals with regard to automatic processing of personal data, accessed to by the Czech Republic in Strasbourg on 8 Sep. 2000 and promulgated under No. 115/2001 Sb.m.s. (the Czech Collection of International Treaties).
83. *See* Act No. 101/2000 Sb., s. 16 subsec. 1, and s. 18 subsec. 1 letter c).
84. *See* Act No. 101/2000 Sb., s. 5 subsec. 2 letter f).

Chapter 2. Freedom to Marry

205. Each 18-year-old person, who is according to legal order of the Czech Republic not yet married, can marry. Younger persons who are at least 16 years old can marry with the approval of the court. Religious obligations of celibacy are relevant only for internal relations in a religious community. Other legal regulations relating to marriage are explored in Part X.

Chapter 3. Freedom of Expression

206. Freedom of expression is guaranteed by the Charter of Fundamental Rights and Freedoms, which is an integral part of the constitutional order of the Czech Republic, namely by Article 17, which reads:

(1) The freedom of expression and the right to information are guaranteed.
(2) Everyone has the right to express his opinion in speech, in writing, in the press, in pictures, or in any other form, as well as to freely seek, receive, and disseminate ideas and information irrespective of the frontiers of the state.
(3) Censorship is not permitted.
(4) The freedom of expression and the right to seek and disseminate information may be limited by law in the case of measures necessary in a democratic society for protecting the rights and freedoms of others, the security of the state, public security, public health, and morality.
(5) State bodies and bodies of local self-government are obliged, in an appropriate manner, to provide information on their activities. Conditions therefor and the implementation thereof shall be provided for by law.

207. The right to freedom of expression is restricted by certain provisions of criminal law which protect human dignity and the beliefs of the faithful against attacks that are inconsistent with constitutionally guaranteed rights. These provisions are dealt with in more detail later in this section, namely in Chapter 8.

208. The right to freedom of expression does not mean the suspension of the internal rules of religious communities which require discipline from their members in both acts and teachings. Those who violate the regulations of religious communities or preach teachings inconsistent with the teachings of their religious community may be, under their internal rules, punished by loss of membership or office, or by loss of access to religious acts. The punishment, however, cannot be enforced through state and other public bodies.

Chapter 4. Due Process Norms and Religious Groups

209. The right to due process is protected under Czech law by the Charter of Fundamental Rights and Freedoms, namely in its Chapter V, headed as 'Right to Judicial and Other Legal Protection' (Articles 36–40). Under Article 36, 'Everyone may assert, through the prescribed procedure, his rights before an independent and impartial court or, in specified cases, before another body.' Other provisions of that chapter contain traditional legal guarantees of the right to due process, such as the right to judicial review of the legality of a decision made by a public administration body (Article 36, section 2), the right to legal aid in proceedings before state authorities and public administration bodies (Article 37, section 2), equality of parties to proceedings (Article 37, section 3), the right to a lawful judge (Article 38, section 1), the application of the principle of no criminal offence, no punishment or other detriment without law (Article 39) and others.

210. As for the relationship between the right to due process and the position of religious communities in the Czech Republic, the Charter of Fundamental Rights and Freedoms, as follows from Article 16 section 2 of the Charter, allows for the restriction of this right. Said provision stipulates that religious communities: 'govern their own affairs; in particular, they establish their own bodies and appoint their own clergy, as well as found religious orders and other church institutions, independent of state authorities'. The autonomy of religious communities results in the non-existence of the possibility to appeal against decisions of bodies of religious communities and their tribunals to state authorities, including state courts. This principle has been affirmed by the case law of the Constitutional Court, which was dealt with in more detail in Part VI, Chapter 2.

Chapter 5. Professional Secrecy

211. The Act expressly stipulates the right 'of ministers to maintain confidentiality with regard to the seal of confession or a right similar to the seal of confession'.[85]This right benefits only ministers who belong to a religious community in which this obligation has been a traditional part of its teachings for at least fifty years.[86]Currently, this includes nineteen religious communities: Roman Catholic Church, Greek Catholic Church, Evangelical Church of Czech Brethren, Czechoslovak Hussite Church, Silesian Evangelical Church A. C., Evangelical Church A. C. in the Czech Republic, Orthodox Church in the Czech Lands, Church of Brethren, Unity of Brethren, Methodist Evangelical Church, Apostolic Church, Unity of Baptist, Old Catholic Church, Seventh-Day Adventists Church, Christian Congregations, Lutheran Evangelical Church A. C. in the Czech Republic, New Apostolic Church, Religious Society of Czech Unitarians, and Church of Jesus Christ of Latter-Day Saints.

212. Ministers of the above-listed religious communities are expressly exempt from the notification duty regarding criminal offences they learn about during a confession or other similar spiritual activity. No investigating, prosecuting or judicial body is allowed to interrogate them on said issues. The ministers testify on said matters neither in criminal proceedings nor in civil proceedings (e.g., matrimonial causes) or administrative proceedings. The provision of the Criminal Code regarding the crime of failing to report an offence does not apply to them (Act No. 40/2009 Sb., the Criminal Code, section 368). The only exception is represented by a statutory duty to foil a future crime. Thus, the ministers may be prosecuted for a crime of failure to foil a criminal offence (Act No. 40/2009 Sb., the Criminal Code, section 367). Based on case law, there has not been a case of conflict in said matters.

85. Act No. 3/2002 Sb., on Churches and Religious Societies, s. 7, subsec. e).
86. *Ibid.*

Chapter 6. Medical Deontology

213. The Czech legal order recognizes the right of medical staff to refuse to render healthcare, should the rendition thereof be inconsistent with their conscience or religious beliefs. The application of said conscientious objection is regulated by Act No. 372/2011 Sb., on Healthcare Services and Conditions for providing them.

214. Euthanasia (an assisted suicide) is not allowed by the Czech legal order. Therefore, conscientious objection is not used in such a case.

215. A case per se is the appointment of a guardian for an ill child whose immediate peril of life requires a blood transfusion and whose parents refuse such medical treatment. The Constitutional Court has dismissed a complaint made by parents – members of the religious society of Jehovah's Witnesses – about the practice of general courts, which have appointed a guardian for their child and committed it to the care of an oncology clinic. In its finding of 20 August 2004 (file No. III. ÚS 459/03), the Constitutional Court came to the conclusion that the protection of the health and life of a child:

> is beyond a doubt a relevant and sufficient reason for the interference in parental rights, as it is a value whose protection within the system of fundamental rights and freedoms is unequivocally a priority. In other words, general courts are bound to safeguard a fair balance between the interests of a child and its parent; special attention shall however be paid to the interest of a child which may, depending on its nature and importance, preponderate over the interest of a parent…; first and foremost, parents shall not be allowed to take measures detrimental to the health or development of a child.

Chapter 7. Non-discrimination

216. Protection against discrimination in the Czech Republic is founded on the constitutional provisions of the Charter of Fundamental Rights and Freedoms (1991). The protection includes 'equality' and 'religious freedom'. Article 3, section 1 of the Charter declares:

> Everyone is guaranteed the enjoyment of their fundamental rights and freedoms without regard to gender, race, colour of skin, language, faith and religion, political or other conviction, national or social origin, membership in a national or ethnic minority, property, birth, or other status.

217. The Czech legal order contains a special regulation regarding anti-discrimination. It is Act No. 198/2009 Sb., the Anti-discrimination Act. In its section 13, the Act assigned the role of an anti-discrimination body to the Public Defender of Rights (the Czech ombudsman), who has the responsibility of combating discrimination on all the grounds covered by the EU Equality Directives 2000/43/EC and 2000/78/EC, including religious discrimination. The Public Defender of Rights is elected by the Chamber of Deputies of the Czech Parliament for a six-year term and is answerable to the Chamber. Candidates are nominated by the Czech president and the Senate. The body is funded from the state budget, through its own independent budget line. The Public Defender of Rights should provide independent assistance to victims of discrimination, undertake research, publish independent reports and exchange information with anti-discrimination bodies in other EU Member States.[87]The office is an independent institution, accountable directly to the Chamber of Deputies of the Parliament. Religious communities have no role in its work.[88]

218. There are several other acts which contain grounds for non-discrimination. Almost all of them provide explicitly for the protection of all inhabitants of the Czech Republic and they make special mention of faith and religion. One of them is the Labour Code, which contains general equality provisions: the right to equal treatment and the prohibition of discrimination apply to all employees.

219. The Czech anti-discrimination provisions implementing the directives cover labour relations, including employment and working conditions, dismissals and pay, and membership and involvement in an organization of workers or employers, in both the public and private sectors. They also cover access to employment (job recruitment, retraining, etc.) which shall be non-discriminatory on all grounds included in the EU anti-discrimination directives – sex, race and ethnicity, religion, disability (state of health), age, and sexual orientation. The Anti-discrimination Act also covers labour relations to which the Labour Code does not apply, such as those of judges, prosecutors, parliament deputies and others. Other areas covered by the Anti-discrimination

87. Act No. 349/1999 Sb., on Public Defender of Rights, s. 21b; Act No. 198/2009 Sb., Anti-discrimination Act, s. 13.
88. Jiří Rajmund Tretera & Záboj Horák, *Czech Republic*, in *Religion and Discrimination Law in the European Union*88–90(ed., Mark Hill QC,Institute for European Constitutional Law, University of Trier 2012).

Act include membership in organizations whose members carry on a particular profession, self-employment, vocational training, and education at all levels. The Anti-discrimination Act also provides protection with respect to access to health, housing, social advantages, and access to goods and services.[89]

220. The Czech Anti-discrimination Act defines direct and indirect discrimination, harassment, sexual harassment, victimization, instruction to discriminate, and incitement to discriminate. The legal system provides for civil, criminal, and administrative enforcement. In civil proceedings, a victim of discrimination can be awarded financial compensation for non-material harm. Criminal prosecution is used only in extreme cases of discrimination. Administrative enforcement consists of sanctioning transgressions and administrative offences. As far as the authors are aware, no cases have as yet been ruled upon concerning discrimination on the grounds of religion or faith.

221. The Anti-discrimination Act permits, under specific conditions, differential treatment in the case of employers who are religious communities. Its section 6, subsection 4 contains the following provision:

222.

A different treatment is [or may be] applied in matters of the right to employment, access to employment or vocation in the case of paid employment performed in churches or religious societies, where, by reason of the nature of such work or the circumstances in which it is carried out, the religious belief, faith or worldview constitutes a genuine, justified and legitimate occupational qualification with respect to the ethos of the church or religious society.

89. *See* the internet site of the European Network of Legal Experts in the Non-discrimination Field, http://www.non-discrimination.net/content/material-scope-14, 14 Dec. 2013.

Chapter 8. Penal Law and Religion

223. Current Czech law does not recognize blasphemy as a crime. The Criminal Code of the Austrian Empire, No. 117/1852, which was in force in the territory of the Czech lands until June 1950, contained a special provision regarding blasphemy and other forms of violation of religion in its section 122. Said code was derogated under the communist regime, namely by the Criminal Code, Act No. 86/1950 Sb., which did not contain any provisions on sanctioning interference with religion. Neither current Criminal Code (Act No. 40/2009 Sb.) contains any provisions on interference with religion.

224. However, effective Czech law contains numerous provisions which protect faithful persons against assaults on their dignity and beliefs. These are the following criminal offences, as stipulated in Act No. 40/2009 Sb., the Criminal Code: restricting the freedom of religion (section 176); defamation of nation, race, ethnicity or another group of persons (section 355); incitement to hatred to a group of persons or restricting their rights and liberties (section 356); genocide (section 400); assault on humanity (section 401); apartheid and discriminating against a group of people (section 402); founding, supporting and promoting a movement aimed at oppressing human rights and liberties (section 403); expressing affection for a movement aimed at oppressing human rights and liberties (section 404); denying, contesting, subscribing to and substantiating genocide (section 405); and the persecution of inhabitants (section 413).

Part VIII. Church Financing

Chapter 1. Direct Financing of Religious Communities

225. In the Czech Republic, religious communities are financed from several resources. They are as follows:

(1) revenues from collections during and outside of church services;
(2) regular contributions and occasional donations by members of religious communities as well as donations by other private entities;
(3) dues paid to religious communities by their members in compliance with the internal rules of said communities;
(4) inheritance and endowments;
(5) proceeds from property (estates, and financial assets) heretofore acquired by religious communities; and
(6) fulfilment under Act No. 428/2012 Sb., on Property Settlement with Churches and Religious Societies.

226. Collections, held either during a church service or after it is over, have always represented a significant part of the income of almost all religious communities. Revenues, therefrom, are comparatively high and relatively stable. They are intended to cover both the costs of worship services and other costs of fundamental units of religious communities or other needs determined by the wishes of the administration of these fundamental units and of their superior bodies (e.g., to support students of theology, to support charities, religious schools and other religious institutes, or to provide social and health aid to victims of floods, earthquakes or other natural disasters). Donations to religious communities may be provided without limitation by private organizations, be it economic (e.g., joint-stock companies and limited liability companies) or civic (e.g., registered associations and non-profit organizations).

227. Some collections cover precisely ascertained future costs, e.g., of the construction, renovation and maintenance of sacral and other buildings; of the reconstruction, conservation and protection of their interiors; and of the acquisition and repair of organs and bells, are also held independently, outside of church services. To serve these needs, there are collection registers placed on the premises of religious communities and requests sent to their members. There are special bodies in certain religious communities that take care of the acquisition and allotment of finance for building and similar purposes, such as Fond bratrské pomoci (Fund of Brotherly Aid) in the Czechoslovak Hussite Church, or Jeronýmova jednota (Jerome's Unity)[90]in the Evangelical Church of Czech Brethren, the analogue of Gustav–Adolf–Werke in Germany and Austria.

228. Some religious communities prescribe, in their internal regulation, the amount to be paid annually as an annual contribution by their members. In some religious communities it is a tithe, while in others it is called religious tax or '*salár*' (i.e., regular annual donation). Neither of these contributions is enforceable through state bodies; still they represent, similarly to collections, a substantial part of the income in most religious communities. A regular contribution has not yet been introduced in the Czech Catholic dioceses; however, similar to a contribution, there are voluntary offerings paid by the believers when requesting to have a Holy Mass celebrated at their intent.

229. Religious communities and their bodies are entitled to testamentary succession like any other subject of law. Under Act No. 89/2012 Sb., the Civil Code, effective as of 1 January 2014, they may also acquire property benefit based on an endowment made in the last will and testament. An endowment is an instrument of law which existed in Czech law until 1950 and which has been renewed by the new Civil Code. Under Czech law, religious communities and their bodies, e.g., monasteries and convents, are not eligible for intestate succession. Therefore, the decedent's last will and testament is necessary so that they become the heirs. Inheritances do not currently represent a significant part of the income of religious communities.

230. Proceeds from their own property are another source of income for religious communities. Apart from interests paid on bank deposits, which constitute a marginal part among those revenues, there are economic gains from real property owned by religious communities. They represented, especially in the past, a great deal of sources for economic security of the activity of religious communities:

> Securing the activity of churches, namely of the Catholic Church, was in the past primarily based on capital contributions of antecedents. They represented assets lawfully acquired by religious legal entities, the assets donated and bequeathed by members of the churches, in particular from the ranks of nobility and bourgeoisie, and in more recent times also from the ranks of less affluent believers.[91]

231. Economic property owned by religious communities was confiscated and transferred to the state as early as during the first year after the communist coup in February 1948. Following the attack on monasteries and the deportation of religious brothers into centralization camps in April 1950, and the subsequent deportation of religious sisters into labour camps, which took place prior to the end of 1952, the buildings of monasteries and convents were also gradually transferred to the state by various legal means. Only churches, chapels, parish buildings and gardens, and some

---

90. It was founded in 1918. Its name derives from Jerome of Prague, Master of Charles University, who was burnt at stake in Constance upon sentence of condemnation passed by the Council, as the second after John Hus, on 30 May 1416.

91. Jiří Rajmund Tretera, *Stát a církve v České republice [State and Churches in the Czech Republic]*120(Karmelitánské nakladatelství 2002).

residential premises – seats of institutions serving religious purposes – remained the private property of religious communities, which still have income from the tenancy of the parts of these buildings.

232. In 1990 and 1991 this property of religious communities was increased by the buildings of monasteries and convents being restored into the ownership of religious orders under Acts No. 298/1990 Sb. and 338/1991 Sb. Those numbered eighty-six male monasteries and eighty-four female convents in the territory of the Czech Republic. Most of their space serves the life and activities of religious orders or religious schools; however, a part of them is used as economic space (flats, retail spaces, lecture, and concert halls), the tenancy of which brings certain gains to the monasteries and convents, although moderate. A deficiency of said acts is that the monasteries and convents were not given back the economic base for the maintenance of their buildings and their activities, at that time.

233. Another restitution regulation is from as late as 2000. It is Act No. 212/2000 Sb., on the Alleviation of certain Property Injustices caused by the Holocaust, passed in favour of the Federation of Jewish Communities. From that time until 2013, no restitution in favour of religious communities came about.

234. It was not until Act No. 428/2012 Sb., on Property Settlement with Churches and Religious Societies, effective as of 1 January 2013, which resolved long postponed issues of alleviation of property injustices.[92]

The Preamble of the Act reads:

> The Parliament, … in an effort to alleviate the consequences of certain property and other injustices brought about by the Communist regime between 1948 and 1989, and to settle property relations between the state and churches and religious societies as a prerequisite of full religious freedom, enabling thereby, through restoration of the property base, the free and independent status of churches and religious societies whose existence and activity it deems as an indispensable feature of a democratic society, has passed the following act…

235. The Act makes possible partial natural restitution and effects financial settlement between the state and religious communities. Further, it introduces an interim provision of allowances to promote the activity of affected religious communities in substitution of state subsidies for salaries of the clergy so far provided by the state. At the same time, the Act repeals Act No. 218/1949 Sb., on the Economic Security of Churches and Religious Societies by the State. It also repeals the present provisions of Act No. 3/2002 Sb. regarding the special right of certain religious communities to state subsidies for the salaries of the clergy.

236. As for the partial natural restitution, certain agricultural and forest estates as well as certain things that the religious communities were dispossessed of in the period from 25 February 1948 to 1 January 1990 shall be returned to the ownership of the religious communities, provided they made a claim, thereto, with the state property administrators, who administered those assets, until 2 January 2014, and adduce evidence of their original ownership. The claims have already been raised by

92. *See* Jiří Rajmund Tretera, *State and Church in the Czech Republic*, in *State and Church in the European Union*51 (ed., Gerhard Robbers, 2nd ednNomos 2005).

religious communities. Only a small portion of claims has been dealt with. The rest must be enforced in the Czech courts. This process is slow and difficult.

237. A more significant part of property settlement shall consist of financial compensation for damages suffered, which is precisely quantified and allotted to individual-affected religious communities in Act No. 428/2012 Sb. Said compensation shall be paid by the state in thirty consecutive yearly instalments. Instalments for years 2013, 2014 and 2015 have already been paid.

238. The third part of the property settlement is the temporary allowance to promote the activity of affected religious communities in substitution of state subsidies for salaries of the clergy so far provided by the state. This allowance shall be paid by the state for the transitional period of seventeen years. In terms of the amount, it shall, for the first three years, correspond to the amount paid to the affected religious communities in 2011. As of the fourth year of the transitional period, the amount of the allowance shall be annually decreased by 5% of the sum paid out in the first year of the transitional period.

Chapter 2. Indirect Financing of Religious Communities

239. Structures owned by religious communities, which serve religious ceremonies or administration, are exempt from real estate tax. Lots in which these structures are located enjoy the same tax-free status.[93]

240. Revenues from church collections, as well as income from religious acts and from members' contributions, are exempt from income taxes.[94]Gratuitous acquisition of property by a registered religious community is exempt from inheritance tax and gift tax.[95]All exemptions from tax duty apply also to bodies of religious communities.

241. Liturgical instruments, which are imported to the Czech Republic by registered religious communities, are not taxed by customs authorities.[96]

93. *See* Act No. 338/1992 Sb., on Real Estate Tax.
94. *See* Act No. 586/1992 Sb., on Income Taxes.
95. *See* Act No. 357/1992 Sb., on Inheritance Tax, Gift Tax and Real Estates Transfer Tax.
96. Decree of the Ministry of Finance No. 247/2002 Sb.

Part IX. Education

Chapter 1. Religious Education in Public and Private Schools

§1. Religious Education in Public Schools

242. Religious education in public schools in the Czech Republic is guaranteed on the constitutional level, namely in Article 16, section 3 of the Charter of Fundamental Rights and Freedoms, which declares that: '… the conditions under which religious education is provided at state schools shall be set by statutes'. Provisions on state schools contained in ensuing education laws apply to all schools named as public. They are either schools founded by a public school authority, i.e., schools founded by territorial self-governing units, particularly municipalities, municipal unions and regions, or schools founded by the state (its central bodies, in particular ministries). Most schools are those founded by territorial self-governing units. Schools founded by the state (ministries) form a minority and are of a specific nature. The state is bound, on the basis of the above-mentioned provision, to adopt a law which imposes and regulates the obligation to provide religious education at schools founded by those founders. This obligation is currently regulated by Act No. 561/2004 Sb., The Education Act.

243. Religious education is taught as a voluntary subject in all grades at schools founded by municipalities, municipal unions and regions, or by the state, be them primary schools (i.e., those at which all the citizens and residents of the Czech Republic complete their compulsory primary education between 6 and 15 years of age) or secondary schools, which follow. The school is obliged to open the voluntary subject of religious education once at least seven pupils have registered for it. To provide religious education, pupils from several grades of one school or even from multiple schools may by joined, not to exceed, however, the number of thirty in one class. Pupils from multiple schools may be joined for the purposes of religious education based on an agreement between the respective schools, which shall also regulate the payment of costs connected with this education.

244. Under Act No. 171/1990 Sb., religious education at schools was secured by all religious communities which had by that time been recognized by the state. As of the effect of Act No. 308/1991 Sb., there were nineteen religious communities listed in the attachment, thereto, as the ones registered in the Czech Republic, and as of the registration of other religious communities in 1993 and 1995, there were twenty-one religious communities. Act No. 3/2002 Sb. restricted the right to provide religious education at schools solely to religious communities registered with a special right to provide such education. The Ministry of Culture, the body qualified to grant the special rights, conferred the right to render religious education to only nine religious communities, which had by then actually exercised their right to such education. Their number has not changed to this day. They are the following religious communities: Roman Catholic Church, Czechoslovak Hussite Church, Evangelical Church of Czech Brethren, Silesian Evangelical Church A. C., Lutheran Evangelical Church A. C. in the Czech Republic, Religious Society of Jehovah's Witnesses, Seventh-Day Adventists Church, Christian Congregations (Darbists), and Apostolic Church (Pentecostals).

245. Religious education at schools is carried out by teachers authorized by any of the above-mentioned religious communities, who are the employees of the school. Several religious communities may agree on the local level that they will authorize a common representative. Act No. 563/2004 Sb., on Pedagogical Staff, sets in section 14, the conditions for enrolment into the teaching staff as a religious education teacher, which are similar to those for other teachers. Further, the Act requires that a religious education teacher has a professional university qualification either in the field of theology or in teaching which is specialized in religious education. A religious education teacher must have valid authorization by a competent body of the respective religious community. In the case of the Roman Catholic Church, such a body is a competent diocese.[97]Should the authorization by a religious community be revoked, the school is obliged to terminate the teacher's employment as a religious education teacher.

246. Religious education classes are attended by pupils who have registered therefor, regardless of whether they belong to the religious community providing religious education or to any other religious community, or whether they are without any denomination. After all, information on pupils' denominations is not and shall not be enquired about at any school, not even at schools founded by religious communities themselves (*see* below).

247. Carrying out religious education at schools does not in any way have an impact on the possibility of religious communities (not only those that have been granted the special right but also all other religious communities) to provide religious education outside the school, i.e., on their own premises. This right, which follows directly from the constitutionally guaranteed religious freedom, is emphasized in Czech legal literature mainly because of the fact that certain religious communities, namely the Roman Catholic Church, were forbidden to provide religious education at parsonages during the time of the totalitarian regime. A minister who would have provided such education or let it be provided in his parish would have been sanctioned for it by having the state permission to exercise religious activity revoked, although religious education at schools unlike religious education at parsonages was allowed.[98]

97. *See* Act No. 561/2004 Sb., the Education Act, s. 15, subsec. 3.

98. For reasons for this seemingly paradoxical attitude by the former regime *see* General Introduction, §3, V.

§2. Religious Education in Religious Schools

248. Religious schools, whose legal status is dealt with in detail in the following chapter, have a special place in the Czech legal order, and they comprise the third category of schools, besides public and private schools. As for religious education at these schools, there are two variants of regulation. Following an agreement with parents who have chosen the school for their children, a school mayimplement compulsory religious education for all pupils. The other alternative is introducing religious education as an optional subject, i.e., one of two or more subjects which a pupil, or theirparents, chooses from.

§3. Religious Education in Private Schools

249. The legal order of the Czech Republic allows individuals and juridical persons other than the state or territorial self-governing units to found schools, which are called private. Private schools are another category of schools in the framework of the state-recognized educational system. The others are public schools and religious schools. All three categories are recorded in the register of schools maintained by the Ministry of Education or, in certain cases, by a region. Private schools are partially financed by the state and partially by other sources, especially from school fees. A private school curriculum is based on the same principles as curricula of public schools; however, the obligation to provide religious education does not apply to them. The founder may or may not include religious education in the curriculum.

250. Private schools may also be founded by religious communities of all types. They may be founded by religious communities registered with a special right to found religious schools as schools different from said religious schools. Then, they may be founded by all other religious communities, be them registered or not.

Chapter 2. Religious Schools

251. Religious schools in the Czech Republic represent a special category of schools, besides public and private schools. In their nature, they rather resemble public schools. There is a principle that legal regulation applicable to public schools, i.e., schools established by municipalities, municipal unions, regions, or the state, applies to religious schools as well, unless the law provides otherwise. The effective Education Act maintains their divergent status from public and private schools, namely from the point of view of financing. Ordinary costs are covered by the state and investment costs by a respective religious community (a body of the religious community that has founded such a school). The religious community usually provides the premises, a property from its own assets, where the school has its seat.

252. During 1949–1950, all religious schools in the territory of the Czech Republic were closed down by the communist state. No sooner than in 1990 were religious schools in the Czech lands renewed, namely on the grounds of Act No. 171/1990 Sb. of 3 May 1990, which amended the then effective Education Act from 1984. Religious schools that have been founded since 1990 are newly established schools. The original religious schools have not been restored. Any religious community that had already been recognized by the state by that time was allowed to establish a religious school. Religious schools can be founded either by a religious community as a whole (headquarters of religious communities) or by bodies of religious communities (dioceses, convents, parishes, congregations of believers), typically in buildings owned by them.

253. When re-establishing religious schools, their founders did not have enough instructors who were at the same time faithful. (During the rule of the communist regime, teachers were trained to perform the role of 'priests of atheism', and active members of religious communities were not accepted, save for rare exceptions, into studies at teachers' colleges.) The founder appointed the head teacher but made it possible to borrow from existing schools teachers who wished to become teachers at religious schools regardless of their denomination or lack of denomination. The only requirement was loyalty to the religious founder, which has endured until this day. The rather swift reestablishment of religious schools, whose number soon drew level with the situation prior to 1950, was also made possible owing to the promptly adopted Acts No. 298/1990 Sb. and 338/1991 Sb., on restitution of a substantial portion of monastery and convent buildings to both male and female religious orders. A great part of these building was used, after being renovated, as buildings to serve the needs of schools founded by religious orders or by other religious entities, e.g., dioceses, to which they were let by the religious orders.

254. Not only teachers at religious schools may be members of various religious communities or be without any denominational affiliation, but also the same applies to pupils who are asked about their religious affiliation neither during the admission proceedings nor at any time thereafter.

255. The interest of the public in having their children educated at religious schools is considerable. It is apparent especially in the case of religious grammar schools, whose number soon exceeded the situation before 1950. To illustrate, in each

Catholic diocese there are, besides grammar schools established by religious orders, between one and three grammar schools founded by the dioceses. Results acquired in certain public surveys attest to the top quality of religious grammar schools.[99]The public also show extraordinary interest in religious preschools.

256. Religious schools, like public and private schools, are founded at all levels but universities. As for their curricula, the religious schools do not differ from public schools, save for minor deviations which are present in the case of public schools as well. It is the following schools which are of great significance: religious preschools for children aged 3–6, religious primary schools for pupils aged 6–15 (education at which is compulsory), eight-year religious grammar schools for students aged 11–19, six-year and four-year grammar schools, vocational schools and academies of music.

257. A particularity of the Czech educational system is higher education schools which admit students who have passed the school leaving examination at grammar school. They are close to universities in their nature, but their students do not obtain academic degrees. Twelve of them have been founded by religious communities as religious schools. They provide theological and other special education. These schools prepare students for careers as teachers of religion at religious preschools or as catechists and pastoral assistants in religious communities, for social work in religious communities as well as in public facilities, and for jobs in journalism. Two examples may be: the Hussite Institute of Theological Studies, which was founded by the Czechoslovak Hussite Church for the training of deacons, pastoral assistants and other members of support staff of this church; JABOK, Religious Higher Social and Pedagogical and Theological School, founded by the Salesian Congregation, for a wide range of social and pedagogic activities of different church and charity bodies.

258. The total number of religious schools in the Czech Republic is 149.[100]Approximately 70% of them were founded by bodies of the Roman Catholic Church, followed by the Evangelical Church of Czech Brethren, and other protestant churches and the Czechoslovak Hussite Church coming after. The Federation of Jewish Communities in the Czech Republic has founded three religious schools.

259. Apart from religious schools, religious communities also establish educational facilities, e.g., religious educational and accommodation facilities, religious facilities for special interest groups' education. There are nineteen of such independently established educational facilities.[101]

260. As time has passed, there have been changes in the Czech legal system regarding the founders of religious schools, similar to those in the regulation of religious

99. In the national assessment of results acquired in the state school leaving exams in June 2011, three religious grammar schools ranked among the ten best grammar schools in the Czech Republic, alongside six public and one private grammar school. This is quite a great number, considering that religious grammar schools only represent a tiny fraction among Czech grammar schools. Cf. Záboj Horák, *Církve a české školství [Churches and the Czech Educational System]*16(Grada 2011).

100. *See* the website of the Ministry of Education, Youth and Sports, Statistická ročenka školství *[Statistical Almanac of Education]* 2015/2016, Chapter A, Vzdělávání v ČR –souhrn *[Education in CR –Summary]*, Chart A 1.1.4 at http://toiler.uiv.cz/rocenka/rocenka.asp, 30 Jun. 2016.

101. *See* the website of the Religious Education Department of the Czech Bishops' Conference. The catalogue of religious schools at http://skolstvi.cirkev.cz/Skoly?kat=6, 30 Jun. 2016.

education at public schools described earlier. Under Act No. 171/1990 Sb., with effect as of 1 June 1990, the right to found religious schools was vested in all religious communities recognized by that time by the state. As of the effect of Act No. 308/1991 Sb., there were nineteen religious communities listed as ones registered in the Czech Republic in the attachment to the Act, and twenty-one in total as of the registration of other religious communities in 1993 and 1995. Act No. 3/2002 Sb. restricted the right to found religious schools to religious communities registered with 'a special' right to establish religious schools. The Ministry of Culture, authorized to grant special rights, accorded the right to found religious schools to only ten religious communities which had indeed exercised their right to establish religious schools before. Their number has not changed since then. The list of these ten communities does not correspond to the list of religious communities that have been granted a special right to provide religious education in public schools. The special right to found religious schools has been given to the following religious communities: Roman Catholic Church, Czechoslovak Hussite Church, Evangelical Church of Czech Brethren, Silesian Evangelical Church A. C., Seventh-Day Adventists Church, Apostolic Church (Pentecostals), Church of Brethren (Evangelical Congregationalists), Unity of Brethren, Unity of Brethren Baptists, and Federation of Jewish Communities in the Czech Republic.

Chapter 3. Theological Schools and Other Theological Studies at Universities

261. The Czech legal system allows neither religious education at universities nor the possibility to found a religious school at the university level. Theology as a science has been traditionally taught at public universities. The Higher Education Act allows that religious communities may found private universities. However, not a single one has done so yet. Religious communities are undoubtedly satisfied with the current existence of five theological schools at public universities.

262. Apart from theological schools, theology is also taught at several other university schools as an optional subject. These are schools focusing on all humanities, natural science and technical studies. Students at those schools who have enrolled in the voluntary subject broaden their general knowledge. It is the schools themselves that decide on enlisting theology into their curricula.

263. Theological schools in the Czech Republic are not independent schools; they are an integral part of public universities. Each university is a legal person with extensive autonomy. Schools, being integral parts of universities, have the right to issue their own constitutions and internal rules, but they do not have legal personality. A provision crucial to the legal status of theological schools is section 33, subsection 4 of Act No. 111/1998 Sb., on Universities, which stipulates that the internal rules of theological schools shall be approved by the academic senate of the university once they have been approved by a relevant religious community, provided the obligation to approve such internal rules is stipulated in the internal regulation of the respective religious community.

264. Currently, there are five theological schools operating in the Czech Republic. Studies at those schools take the form of either bachelor or master studies followed by two other degrees – licentiate and doctorate, the award of which is regulated differently depending on confession. There are three theological schools at Charles University in Prague.

265. The Catholic Theological School of Charles University, one of the four founding schools, has been a part of the university since its establishment in 1348. Besides preparing candidates of priesthood from Roman Catholic dioceses in Bohemia and from some religious orders from the whole territory of the country, there are numerous lay undergraduates studying theology regardless of their denomination. Further, other fields of study were opened at the school a few years ago, namely the history of Christian arts, the history of European culture, and applied ethics.

266. In 1990, the Evangelical Theological School was incorporated into Charles University, which offers courses to candidates of preacher posts in the Evangelical Church of Czech Brethren and a further more than ten protestant churches in the Czech lands, as well as to prospective lay workers in the field of social work and teaching from various churches, and to those interested in the study regardless of their denomination. The Evangelical Theological School of Charles University is not tightly connected with any religious community; both the teaching staff and students are comprised of mixed confessions.

267. In 1990, the Hussite Theological School was incorporated into Charles University. It offers studies to candidates of priesthood in the Czechoslovak Hussite Church and in the Old Catholic Church, as well as to candidates of preacher posts in the Religious Society of Czech Unitarians. Recently, the Institute of Jewish Studies and the Department of Eastern Christianity have been opened. There are also numerous prospective lay workers of various religious communities in the field of social work and teaching, and anyone interested in the studies regardless of their denomination. A broad ecumenical openness is given by the diverse denominational affiliation of both students and teachers. Despite this openness, the school is fundamentally connected mainly with the current theology of the Czechoslovak Hussite Church.

268. Three theological schools, which are an integral part of Charles University in Prague, cooperate with one another as well as with other university schools. Some students choose subjects taught at various schools at the same time.

269. Palacký University in Olomouc encompasses the Saints Cyril and Methodius School of Theology, which is concerned with Catholic theology. Besides preparing candidates of priesthood from Roman Catholic dioceses in Moravia and Silesia, and from some religious orders from the whole territory of the country, there are numerous lay undergraduates. What is frequent is a course with two fields of study, run in cooperation with other university schools, in particular in the field of a teacher of religious education and a language instructor (primarily English and German).

270. In 1991, the Theological School of the University of South Bohemia in České Budějovice, which is concerned with Catholic theology, was established. The school does not serve the preparation of candidates of the priesthood but prepares professionally teachers of religious education, pastoral assistants and other social workers. Members of the teaching staff are of different denominations. The most numerous among Catholics are members of the Salesian congregation. The school tightly cooperates with the theological institute in Benediktbeuern (Bavaria).

271. There were 3,300 students at the Catholic theological schools[102]and more than 1,000 students at the Evangelical and Hussite theological schools in the academic year 2011–2012. Candidates of ministry are only a minority among the students at all five theological schools. All Czech theological schools have features of considerable declericalization. Most students at all theological schools are women.

102. Česká biskupská konference (ed.,) [The Czech Bishops' Conference (ed.,)], *Katolická církev v České republice [Catholic Church in the Czech Republic]*72(Karmelitánské nakladatelství 2013).

Part X. Matrimonial and Family Law

Chapter 1. Legal Position of Religious Marriage

272. The betrothed (those who enter into marriage: a bride and groom) have the right in the Czech Republic to freely choose if they will solemnize a valid marriage either in civil or in religious form, both of which are equal. This system is referred to as alternative forms of solemnization of marriage in Czech legal theory. Publicly valid marriages entered into before bodies of religious communities are termed 'religious marriages' in Czech legal regulations, regardless of whether the religious community is a Christian one or one other than Christian. The principle of the alternative forms of marriage is traditional in the territory of the Czech lands.

273. The principle of alternative forms of solemnization of marriage applied in the Czech lands as well as in other states of Cisleithan Regions of the Austro–Hungarian Empire already in the time of the effectiveness of basic state laws called 'the December Constitution' (1867), or regulations implementing the Constitution. The December Constitution remained in force in the Czech lands until the foundation of the independent Czechoslovak state on 28 October 1918, and the regulation on forms of marriage, based on the reception of the existing Austrian legal order, until 13 June 1919. Between 1868 and 1919, a completely free choice between civil and religious marriage concerned only persons of non-Catholic denominations or those without any denominational affiliation. The freedom was limited in the case of Catholics, who should have preferentially solemnized a religious marriage; only if the minister refused to wed them for reasons not stipulated in the state law were they entitled to enter into a civil marriage, which implies that in the case of Catholics, a civil marriage was only a subsidiary form.

274. The principle of an unlimited choice of alternative forms of marriage was implemented to the full extent a few months after the foundation of the independent Czechoslovak state. It happened by Act No. 320/1919 Sb. of 22 May 1919, effective from 13 June 1919, which amended civil-law provisions on solemnities of contracting a marriage, on the dissolution of marriage and on impediments of marriage. The legal regulation under said law remained in force until 1 January 1950.

275. During the Nazi occupation (1939–1945), the above-mentioned regulation only benefited the Czechs living in the occupied inland, the so-called Protectorate Bohemia and Moravia. Regarding Germans and other Reich citizens in the inland and borderlands, the obligatory civil marriage was introduced by the occupiers. A part of the wedding ceremony for Germans were then manifestations connected with an emphasis on the Nazi ideology concerning the duties of parents – members of 'the higher race', in relation to a 'New Europe' conquered and built by the Nazis.

276. After the liberation of Czechoslovakia in 1945, the application of alternative forms of marriage was returned to in the entire territory of the state within its original borders. The doctrine of legal continuity of the Czechoslovak legal order, effective as of 30 September 1938, was upheld.

277. The effectiveness of alternative forms of marriage was discontinued in Czechoslovakia no sooner than under the dictatorship of the Communist Party, which assumed power through a coup on 25 February 1948. The obligatory civil marriage was introduced by Act No. 265/1949 Sb., on Family Law, effective as of 1 January 1950. This position was affirmed by Act No. 94/1963 Sb., on Family (The Family Act).

278. After the restoration of democracy, the Czech legal order once again returned to alternative forms of marriage. The change was introduced in the entire territory of the Czech and Slovak Federative Republic, effective as of 1 July 1992, by Act No. 234/1992 Sb., to Amend Act No. 94/1963 Sb., on Family, adopted by the then Federal Assembly.

279. In the period between 2001 and 2012, in the course of the preparation of the New Civil Code, which was to replace among others the present Family Act, there was a stormy public debate on the topic of the solemnization of marriage – whether to keep the alternative forms of marriage or to introduce obligatory civil marriage – which resulted in a decision to maintain the present situation. On 3 February 2012, the Parliament of the Czech Republic adopted Act No. 89/2012 Sb., the Civil Code, to come into effect on 1 January 2014, which keeps the alternative forms of the solemnization of marriage, apart from a minor change discussed hereinafter.

280. Until 1 January 1950, it was possible to solemnize marriage in Czechoslovakia before any state-recognized religious community. This situation was returned to as of 1 July 1992 by Act No. 234/1992 Sb. on the understanding that the term 'recognition' was replaced by the term 'registration' the year before. It was possible to solemnize the marriage before all religious communities registered under Act No. 308/1991 Sb., on Freedom of Religious Belief and on the Position of Churches and Religious Societies. Those were the nineteen religious communities stated in the attachment to the Act No. 308/1991 Sb., including the other two religious communities registered under said law later on (1993, 1995).

281. According to Act No. 3/2002 Sb., on Churches and Religious Societies, which liberalized the conditions of registration of religious communities, the right to solemnize religious marriages is solely held by religious communities registered with 'special rights'. It benefits all twenty-one religious communities registered earlier and listed in the attachment thereto. None of the fifteen religious communities registered later (2002–2013) has yet qualified for the registration with 'special rights'. As soon as any of them (or any other religious community that will be registered in the future) qualifies, it will gain the right to registration with 'special rights' inclusive of the right to solemnize religious marriages. This right is gained by a religious community in an administrative proceeding that may be appealed against to a court.

282. Act No. 234/1992 Sb. prescribes that a marriage is entered into by the affirmative declaration of a man and a woman before a state body or the body of a religious community that they enter into marriage with one another, which is made solemnly in public, in the presence of two witnesses. The betrothed must meet all requirements for the solemnization of marriage stipulated by law. According to Act No. 91/1998 Sb., to Amend Act No. 94/1963 Sb., on Family, the betrothed shall, prior to a contemplated religious marriage, obtain a certificate issued by a public registry office proving that they are capable of entering into marriage in compliance with the legal order of the Czech Republic. Such a certificate shall not on the day of a religious marriage exceed three months from its issuance. Failing to meet this condition constitutes civil nullity of the marriage. As of its effectiveness on 1 January 2014, the New Civil Code, i.e., Act No. 89/2012 Sb., prolonged said period to six months.

283. Under current legislation, the wedding minister is, in the case of a religious marriage, obliged to deliver within three working days a record of the solemnization of the marriage to a registry in whose administrative district the marriage was entered into. Publicly valid documents of the solemnization of marriage will be issued by the registry.

284. If a civil marriage has been solemnized, any ensuing religious ceremonies have no legal effects. If a religious marriage with civil-law effects has been solemnized, a civil marriage cannot be entered into subsequently (Act No. 89/2012 Sb., section 670).

Chapter 2. Legal Position of Religious Family Law

285. All religious communities are entitled to use their own ecclesiastical law when it comes to their internal affairs, thus also ecclesiastical family law. However, this law is only enforceable internally, in individual religious communities, through their own legal sanctions; it is not enforceable by the state.

286. Decisions by bodies of religious communities in matrimonial matters, inclusive of declaring the marriage null and void, have no effects outside of the respective religious community.

287. None of the religious communities shall be forced to carry out marriage ceremonies.

Part XI. Religion and Culture

Chapter 1. Religion and Art

288. Religious communities are important upholders of cultural functions in the country. Religious organizations look after thousands of historical monuments and modern dominant features of towns and villages, such as churches, parish houses, monasteries and other buildings, including their richly decorated interiors. Religious communities also play an important part in national music life, in many library, archival and museum activities, and in the public education system through both their own religious schools of all grades and the teaching of religion at public elementary and secondary schools.[103]

289. The protection of monuments in the Czech Republic is regulated by Act No. 20/1987 Sb., on State Monument Care, which does not contain any special provision on religious communities. The owner is obliged to maintain the monument in a proper condition and is subject to a series of other restrictions. However, the owner can apply for state subsidies for renovation and can also obtain subsidies from regional and communal authorities.

103. *See* Jiří Rajmund Tretera, Záboj Horák, *The Mutual Roles of Religion and State in Czech Republic*, in *The Mutual Roles of Religion and State in Europe*35(ed., Balázs Schanda,Institute for European Constitutional Law, University of Trier 2013).

Chapter 2. Religion and Media

290. The execution of state administration in the field of radio and television broadcasting is regulated by Act No. 231/2001 Sb., on Radio and Television Broadcasting Operation. The Act imposes a duty on the operator to secure that broadcasted programmes do not incite hatred on the basis of gender, race, colour of skin, language, faith and religion, political and other views, national or social origin, nationality and ethnicity, wealth, and family or other status. The operator of radio and television broadcasting may not further put on programmes which may strengthen stereotype prejudice regarding ethnic, religious or racial minorities. The operatoris also not permitted to put on religious or atheistic business messages, or messages attacking faith, religion or political and other views. Radio and television broadcasts of church services cannot be interrupted by commercials or teleshopping. Commercials and teleshopping shall not be presented on a split screen during the television broadcast of church services.

291. Regarding religious broadcast, the cooperation with religious communities is contractually secured only on a public station – Czech Radio. Czech Television also has religious broadcasts, however, without a contract entered into with religious communities.[104]

104. *See* Part III, Ch. 4, §5, V.

Chapter 3. Religion and Civil Society

292. Under the constitutional principles of the Czech Republic, the state may be bound neither to an exclusive ideology, inclusive of atheism, nor to a particular religious faith (the Charter of Fundamental Rights and Freedoms, Article 2, section 1). It, however, does not exclude the joint presence of representatives of the state, including regions and municipalities, and religious communities at celebrations of national and public importance. To illustrate, the president of the state has several times attended religious celebrations on the national festivals of St. Wenceslas, Master John Hus and Saints Cyril and Methodius, having his own speech at times.[105]However, Catholic bishops conducted the funeral of ex-President Václav Havel in December 2011, which, however, happened at the request of his relatives, not upon a call by state bodies. If a president was a member of another religious community, nothing would hinder a funeral conducted by representatives of that religious community, provided he and his family so wished. This tradition has endured since the time of the first Czechoslovak Republic (the evangelical funeral of President T. G. Masaryk in September 1937). It also does not contravene the constitutional principles of religious neutrality of the state if the president elect asks religious officials for either the prayer Te Deum or another prayer by which the success of his office is impetrated and at which he is present. It depends solely on his personal wish as to whether or not such a ceremony will take place. Joint celebrations are often connected with ecumenical or interreligious attendance.

293. The involvement of representatives of religious communities in the care of inmates, members of the police and fire rescue service, victims of disasters and acts of violence organized by a civil society, was dealt with in Part III, Chapter 4, §5. Their participation in public education was discussed in Part IX.

105. Jiří Rajmund Tretera, Záboj Horák, *The Mutual Roles of Religion and State in Czech Republic*, in *The Mutual Roles of Religion and State in Europe*33–34 (ed., Balázs Schanda,Institute for European Constitutional Law, University of Trier, 2013).

Chapter 4. Religion and Public Debate

294. Religious communities do not enjoy statutorily guaranteed engagement in the preparation of legislation. They express their opinion on public affairs based on a constitutionally protected freedom of expression, just like other entities and individuals, in public press or by other suitable means, inclusive of the right to petition. On certain, rare occasions their representatives were invited to work in expert committees established by central state bodies, e.g., in the period 1999–2001, to work on a draft of a statute regarding churches and religious societies, which was later published as Act No. 3/2002 Sb. A case sui generis was the participation of the Conference of Religious Superiors in the preparation of Acts No. 298/1990 Sb. and 338/1991 Sb., which returned to the ownership of monasteries and convents part of their buildings. Another example would be the attendance of representatives of seventeen religious communities in the Czech Republic at talks with the government regarding the preparation of the Act on Property Settlement with Religious Communities, No. 428/2012 Sb., which took place between 2010 and 2011; it was concluded by an agreement on 25 August 2011.

Selected Bibliography

General and Comprehensive References
Hrdina, Antonín Ignác. *Náboženská svoboda v právu České republiky* [Religious Liberty in the Legal System of the Czech Republic]. Praha: Eurolex Bohemia, 2004.
Jäger, Petr. *Církve a náboženské společnosti v České republice a jejich právní postavení* [Churches and Religious Societies in the Czech Republic and Their Legal Status]. Brno: CDK, 2006.
Němec, Damián. *Concordat Agreements Between the Holy See and the Post-Communist Countries (1990–2010)*. Leuven–Paris–Walpole, MA: Peeters, 2012.
Potz, Richard, Brigitte Schinkele, Karl Schwarz, Eva Maria Synek & Wolfgang Wieshaider (eds.). *Recht und Religion in Mittel- und Osteuropa, Band 2: Tschechien* [Law and Religion in Central and Eastern Europe, Volume 2: Czech Republic]. Coordinated by Jiří Rajmund Tretera & Wolfgang Wieshaider. Wien: WUV Universitätsverlag, 2004.
Přibyl, Stanislav. *Tschechisches Staatskirchenrecht nach 1989* [Czech Religion Law after 1989]. Brno: L. Marek, 2010.
Riobó Serván, Alfonso. *El derecho de libertad religiosa en la República Checa y en la República Eslovaca* [Law on Religious Freedom in the Czech Republic and Slovak Republic]. Madrid: Dykinson, S. L., 2005.
Tretera, Jiří Rajmund. *Stát a církve v České republice* [State and Churches in the Czech Republic]. Kostelní Vydří: Karmelitánské nakladatelství, 2002.
Tretera, Jiří Rajmund & Záboj Horák.*Konfesní právo.* [Religion Law].Praha: Leges, 2015.
Tretera, Jiří Rajmund & Záboj Horák. *Slovník církevního práva* [Dictionary of Church Law]. Praha: Grada Publishing, a. s., 2011.
Valeš, Václav. *Konfesní právo. Průvodce studiem* [Religion Law, Study Guide]. Plzeň: Aleš Čeněk, 2008.
References in Foreign Languages
References in English Language
Horák, Záboj. *'Religion and the Secular State in the Czech Republic'* in *Religion and the Secular State: National Reports, Reports Issued for the Occasion of XVIIIth Congress of the International Academy of Comparative Law*, edited by Javier Martínez-Torrón & Cole W. Durham. Madrid: Servicio de Publicaciones Facultad de Derecho Universidad Complutense de Madrid in cooperation with The International Center for Law and Religion Studies, J. Reuben Clark Law School, Brigham Young University, USA, 2015, 234–247.
Tretera, Jiří Rajmund. '*Concordatarian Agreements and Public Agreements in the Czech State Ecclesiastical Law*'in *Religion and Law in Dialogue: Covenantal and Non-covenantal Cooperation Between State and Religion in Europe*, edited by Richard Puza & Norman Doe. Leuven–Paris–Dudley: Peeters, 2006, 33–38.

Tretera, Jiří Rajmund. '*Czech State Ecclesiastical Law at the Beginning of the 21st Century*' in *Czech Law Between Europeanization and Globalization, New Phenomena in Law at the Beginning of the 21st Century*, edited by Michal Tomášek. Praha: Charles University in Prague, Karolinum Press, 2010, 68–76.
Tretera, Jiří Rajmund. '*Church and State in the Czech Republic*' in*European Journal for Church and State Research* 7 (2000): 299–315.
Tretera, Jiří Rajmund. '*Church and State in the Czech Republic*' in*European Journal for Church and State Research* 8 (2001): 287–294.
Tretera, Jiří Rajmund. '*Church and State in the Czech Republic in 2001* 'in *European Journal for Church and State Research* 9 (2002): 291–295.
Tretera, Jiří Rajmund. '*Church Autonomy in the Czech Republic*' in *Church Autonomy: A Comparative Survey*, edited by Gerhard Robbers. Frankfurt am Main: Peter Lang, 2001, 633–644.
Tretera, Jiří Rajmund. '*Legal Status of the Islamic Minority in the Czech Republic*' in *Islam in Europe*. Bratislava: Ústav pre vzťahy štátu a cirkví, 2005, 300–306.
Tretera, Jiří Rajmund, '*Religious Entities as Legal Persons – Czech Republic*' in *Churches and Other Religious Organisations as Legal Persons*, edited by Lars Friedner. Leuven–Paris–Dudley, MA: Peeters, 2007, 55–59.
Tretera, Jiří Rajmund. '*State and Church in the Czech Republic*' in *Law and Religion in Post-Communist Europe*, edited by Silvio Ferrari & Cole W. Durham. Leuven: Peeters, 2003, 81–97.
Tretera, Jiří Rajmund. '*State and Church in the Czech Republic*' in *State and Church in the European Union,* 2nd ed., edited by Gerhard Robbers. Baden-Baden: Nomos, 2005, 35–54.
Tretera, Jiří Rajmund. '*Systems of Relations Between the State and Churches in General and Their Occurrence in the Czech Lands in Particular*' in *Many Cultures, Many Faces, Monsignor W. Onclin Chair*. Leuven: Katholieke Universiteit Leuven, 2002, 31–56.
Tretera, Jiří Rajmund. '*The Czech Bishop's Conference and the Process of Democratization in the Czech Republic*' in *Chiesa cattolica ed Europa centro-orientale, Libertà religiosa e processo di democratizzazione* [The Catholic Church and Central-Eastern Europe, Religious Freedom and the Process of Democratization], edited by Antonio G. Chizzoniti. Milano: Vita e Pensiero, 2004, 45–107, 551–605.
Tretera, Jiří Rajmund. '*The Principles of State Ecclesiastical Law in the Czech Republic* 'in *Le statut des confessions religieuses des États candidats à l'Union européenne* [The Status of Religions in the Candidate States of the European Union], edited by Francis Messner. Milano: Giuffrè, 2002, 139–156.
Tretera, Jiří Rajmund & Záboj Horák. '*Czech Republic*' in *Religion and Discrimination Law in the European Union (La discrimination en matière religieuse dans l'Union Européenne)*, edited by Mark Hill. Trier: Institute for European Constitutional Law, University of Trier, on behalf of the European Consortium for Church and State Research, 2012.
Tretera, Jiří Rajmund & Záboj Horák. '*Immigration and Religion in the Czech Republic*' in *Immigration, National and Regional Laws and Freedom of Religion*, edited by Agustín Motilla. Leuven: Peeters, 2012, 35–44.

Selected Bibliography

Tretera, Jiří Rajmund & Záboj Horák. '*Religion and Criminal Law: The Czech Republic*' in *Religion and Criminal Law/Religion et Droit Pénal*, edited by Matti Kotiranta & Norman Doe. Leuven–Paris–Walpole, MA: Peeters, 2013, 41–47.

Tretera, Jiří Rajmund & Záboj Horák. '*Religion in Public Education in the Czech Republic*' in *Religion in Public Education/La religion dans l'éducation publique*, edited by Gerhard Robbers. Trier: European Consortium for Church and State Research, 2011, 99–112.

Tretera, Jiří Rajmund & Záboj Horák. '*The Application of the Freedom of Religion Principles of the European Convention on Human Rights in the Czech Republic*' in *Religious Freedom in the European Union*, edited by Achilles Emilianides. Leuven: Peeters, 2011, 99–103.

Tretera, Jiří Rajmund & Záboj Horák. '*The Financing of Religious Communities in the Czech Republic*' in *Financing of Religious Communities in the European Union*, edited by Brigitte Basdevant-Gaudemet & Salvatore Berlingò. Leuven: Peeters, 2009, 119–128.

Tretera, Jiří Rajmund & Záboj Horák. '*The Mutual Roles of Religion and State in Czech Republic*' in *The Mutual Roles of Religion and State in Europe*, edited by Balázs Schanda. Trier: Institute for European Constitutional Law, University of Trier, on behalf of the European Consortium for Church and State Research, 2013, 33–41.

Tretera, Jiří Rajmund & Záboj Horák. '*Public Authorities and the Training of Religious Personnel in Europe – Report Czech Republic*' in *Public Authorities and the Training of Religious Personnel in Europe*, edited by Francis Messner. Granada: Editorial Comares, 2015, 183–194.

Tretera, Jiří Rajmund & Záboj Horák. '*Religious Jurisdictions in the Czech Republic*' in *Jurisdictions religieuses et l'Etat – Religious Adjudication and the State*, edited by Richard Potz & Wolfgang Wieshaider. Granada: Editorial Comares, 2015, 195–202.

References in Other Foreign Languages

Horák, Záboj. '*Information über die Situation in der Tschechischen Republik*' [Information about the Situation in the Czech Republic]in *Die finanziellen Rahmenbedingungen kirchlichen Handelns* [Financial Frame Conditions for Church Activities], edited by Burkhard Kämper & Hans-Werner Thönnes. Essener Gespräche zum Thema Staat und Kirche 47 (2013): 122.

Horák, Záboj. '*République tchèque*' [Czech Republic]in *Dictionnaire du Droit des Religions* [Dictionary of Law on Religions]. Edited by Francis Messner. Paris: CNRS Editions, 2011, 620–625.

Horák, Záboj. '*Zur rechtlichen Situation der Theologischen Fakultäten in Tschechien*' [On the Legal Situation of the Theological Schools in the Czech Republic]in *Neuere Entwicklungen im Religionsrecht europäischer Staaten* [New Developments in Religion Law in European States], edited by Wilhelm Rees, María Roca & Balázs Schanda. Berlin: Duncker & Humblot, 2013, 293–301.

Tretera, Jiří Rajmund. '*Die jüngsten Rechtsfragen des tschechischen Religionsrechts, Teil 1*' [The Most Recent Legal Issues of the Czech Religion Law]. *Österreichisches Archiv für Recht und Religion* [Austrian Archives for Law and Religion] 2 (2002): 230–238.

Tretera, Jiří Rajmund. '*Finansowanie Kościołów w Republice Czeskiej*' [Financing of Churches in the Czech Republic]in *Systemy finansowania instytucji kościelnych w Europie [Systems of Financing of Church Institutions in Europe]*, edited by Józef Krukowski. Lublin: Towarzystwo Naukowe Katolickiego Uniwersytetu Lubelskiego, 2000, 109–122.

Tretera, Jiří Rajmund. '*Chiesa e Stato nella Repubblica Ceca*' [Church and State in the Czech Republic]in *Diritto e religione nell' Europa post-comunista* [Law and Religion in the Post-Communist Europe], edited by Silvio Ferrari & Cole W. Durham & Elizabeth A. Sewell. Bologna: Mulino, 2004, 107–131.

Tretera, Jiří Rajmund. '*Kirche und Sozialismus in der Tschechoslowakei 1948–1989*' [Church and Socialism in Czechoslovakia 1948–1989]in *Kirche und Sozialismus in Osteuropa* [Church and Socialism in Eastern Europe], edited by Jana Osterkamp & Renate Schulze. Wien: Facultas WUV, 2007, 58–70.

Tretera, Jiří Rajmund. '*Państwo i kościół w Czechach*' [State and Church in the Czech Republic]in *Państwo i kościół w krajach Unii Europejskiej* [State and Church in the Countries of the European Union], edited by Gerhard Robbers. Wrocław: Kolonia, Spółka z o.o., 2007, 67–80.

Tretera, Jiří Rajmund. '*Rechtliche und wirtschaftliche Grundlagen für den Dienst der Kirchen*' [Legal and Economic Bases for the Service of Churches]in *Gemeinsame Wege – getrennte Wege (Die Zukunft der Beziehungen zwischen Staat und Kirchen)* [Common Ways – Separate Ways (The Future of Relations Between State and Churches)]. Praha: Konrad–Adenauer–Stiftung, 1996, 75–85.

Tretera, Jiří Rajmund. '*Religia i edukacja w Europie Środkowo–Wschodniej*' [Religion and Education in Central–Eastern Europe]in *Kultura i prawo, Religia i wolność religijna w Unii Europejskiej* [Culture and Law, Religion and Religious Freedom in the European Union], edited by Józef Krukowski & Otto Theisen. Lublin: Towarzystwo Naukowe Katolickiego Uniwersytetu Lubelskiego, 2003, 98–119.

Tretera, Jiří Rajmund. '*Religia i wolność religijna w Republice Czeskiej*' [Religion and Religious Freedom in the Czech Republic]in *Kultura i prawo. Religia i wolność religijna w państwach Europy środkowo–wschodniej w perpektywie integracji europejskiej* [Culture and Law, Religion and Religious Freedom in the States of Central–Eastern Europe in the Perspective of the European Integration], edited by Józef Krukowski. Lublin: Towarzystwo Naukowe Katolickiego Uniwersytetu Lubelskiego, 2004, 129–142.

Tretera, Jiří Rajmund. '*Religion und Ausbildung in Mittel– und Osteuropa*' [Religion and Education in Central and Eastern Europe]in *Kultur und Recht, Religion und Religionsfreiheit in der Europäischen Union* [Culture and Law, Religion and Religious Freedom in the European Union], edited by Józef Krukowski & Otto Theisen. Lublin: Wissenschaftliche Gesellschaft der Katholischen Universität Lublin, 2003, 103–111.

Tretera, Jiří Rajmund. '*Religion und Religionsfreiheit in der Tschechischen Republik*' [Religion and Religious Freedom in the Czech Republic]in *Kultur und Recht, Religion und Religionsfreiheit in den Ostmitteleuropas Staaten in der Perspektive der Integration mit EU* [Culture and Law, Religion and Religious Freedom in the States of Central–Eastern Europe in the Perspective of the European Integration], edited by Józef Krukowski. Lublin: Wissenschaftliche Gesellschaft der Katholischen Universität Lublin, 2004, 139–154.

Selected Bibliography

Tretera, Jiří Rajmund. '*Slowakei, Tschechische Republik*' [Slovakia, Czech Republic] in *Lexikon für Kirchen– und Staatskirchenrecht, Band 2 [Lexicon of Church Law and Religion Law. Volume 2]*, edited by Axel Freiherr von Campenhausen, Ilona Riedel-Spangenberger & Reinhold Sebott. Paderborn–WienMünchenZürich: Ferdinand Schöningh, 2002, 453–454, 455–457.

Tretera, Jiří Rajmund. '*Staat und Kirche in der Tschechischen Republik*' [State and Church in the Czech Republic]in *Staat und Kirche in der Europäischen Union* [State and Church in the European Union], edited by Gerhard Robbers. Baden-Baden: Nomos, 2005, 37–58.

Tretera, Jiří Rajmund & Záboj Horák. '*Das Verhältnis von Staat und Kirche in Tschechien*' [Relation of State and Church in the Czech Republic]. *Zeitschrift für Evangelisches Kirchenrecht [*Review for Evangelical Church Law*]* 52–3(2007): 571–577.

Tretera, Jiří Rajmund & Záboj Horák. '*Die theologische Ausbildung in der Tschechischen Republik*' [Theological Education in the Czech Republic]in *Theologische Fakultäten an europäischen Universitäten, Rechtliche Situation und theologische Perspektiven* [Theological Schools at European Universities, Legal Situation and Theological Perspectives], edited by Adrian Loretan. Münster: LIT–Verlag, 2004, 155–161.

Tretera, Jiří Rajmund & Záboj Horák. '*Historische und Rechtliche Aspekte des Religionsunterrichts in Tschechien*' [Historical and Legal Aspects of Religious Education in the Czech Republic]in *Historische und rechtliche Aspekte des Religionsunterrichts, Wissenschaft und Religion, Band 8 [Historical and Legal Aspects of Religious Education, Science and Religion, Volume 8]*, edited by Alfred Rinnerthaler. Frankfurt am Main: Peter Lang, 2004, 413–416.

Wieshaider, Wolfgang. '*Gesellschaftliche Rahmenbedingungen, Strafrecht, Summary*' [Social Framework, Criminal Law, Summary]in *Recht und Religion in Mittel– und Osteuropa. Band II – Tschechien* [Law and Religion in Central and Eastern Europe. Volume II – Czech Republic], edited by Potz,Richard, Brigitte Schinkele, Karl Schwarz, Eva Maria Synek & Wolfgang Wieshaider; coordinated by Jiří Rajmund Tretera & Wolfgang Wieshaider. Wien: Universitätsverlag, 2004, 13–18, 136–154.

Commentaries

Jäger, Petr & Aleš Chocholáč. *Zákon o majetkovém vyrovnání s církvemi a náboženskými společnostmi. Komentář*. [Act on Property Settlement with Churches and Religious Societies. Commentary]. Praha: Wolters Kluwer, 2015.

Kříž, Jakub. *Zákon o církvích a náboženských společnostech. Komentář* [Act on Churches and Religious Societies. Commentary]. Praha: C. H. Beck, 2011.

Kříž, Jakub & Václav Valeš. *Zákon o majetkovém vyrovnání s církvemi a náboženskými společnostmi. Komentář* [Act on Property Settlement with Churches and Religious Societies. Commentary]. Praha: C. H. Beck, 2013.

Books

Čornej, Petr & Jiří Pokorný. *A Brief History of the Czech Lands*. Praha: Práh, 2003.

Filipi, Pavel (ed.). *Malá encyklopedie evangelických církví* [Small Encyclopaedia of Evangelical Churches]. Praha: Libri, 2008.

Gerloch, Aleš. *Teorie práva [Theory of Law]*, 4th ed. Plzeň: Aleš Čeněk, 2007.

Horák, Záboj. *Církve a české školství. Právní zajištění působení církví a náboženských společností ve školství na území českých zemí od roku 1918 do současnosti* [Churches and the Czech Educational System. Legal Conditions of the Involvement of Churches and Religious Societies in Education in the Territory of the Czech Lands from 1918 until Today]. Praha: Grada Publishing, a.s., 2011.

Horák, Záboj. *Církve a školství. Vybrané dokumenty ke studiu českého konfesního práva* [Churches and the Educational System. Selected Documents for the Study of Czech Religion Law]. Praha: Univerzita Karlova v Praze, Právnická fakulta, 2012.

Kříž, Jakub (ed.). *Náboženství a veřejná moc v zemích Evropské unie* [Religion and Public Authority in European Union Countries]. Praha: Ministerstvo kultury České republiky, 2009.

Pavlíček, Václav (ed.). *Ústavní právo a státověda, II. díl, Ústavní právo České republiky* [Constitutional Law and Political Science, Volume II, Constitutional Law of the Czech Republic]. Praha: Leges, 2011.

Spratek, Daniel. *Evropská ochrana náboženské svobody* [European Protection of Religious Freedom]. Brno: L. Marek, 2008.

Václavík, David. *Náboženství a moderní česká společnost* [Religion and Modern Czech Society]. Praha: Grada, 2010.

Valeš, Václav. *Restituce církevního majetku v České republice po roce 1989* [Restitution of Church Property in the Czech Republic after 1989]. Brno: Moravsko-slezská křesťanská akademie, 2009.

Articles

Articles in Books

Jäger, Petr. '*Svoboda vyznání a právní poměry církví a náboženských společností v letech 1948–1989*' [Freedom of Belief and Legal Status of Churches and Religious Societies in 1948–1989]in *Komunistické právo v Československu* [Communist Law in Czechoslovakia], edited by Michal Bobek, Pavel Molek & Vojtěch Šimíček. Brno: Masarykova univerzita, Mezinárodní politologický ústav, 2009, 769–810.

Tretera, Jiří Rajmund. '*Konfesní právo v Českých zemích*' [Religion Law in the Czech Lands]in *Ius et Iustitia, Acta VII. et VIII. Symposii Iuris Canonici*, edited by Peter Holec. Spišská Kapitula-Spišské Podhradie: Kňazský seminár biskupa Jána Vojtaššáka, 2004, 117–127.

Tretera, Jiří Rajmund. '*Zákon o církvích a náboženských společnostech a rozvoj českého konfesního práva na počátku 21. století*' [The Act on Churches and Religious Societies and the Development of Czech Religion Law at the Beginning of the 21st Century]in *Nové jevy v právu na počátku 21. století [*New Phenomena in Law at the Beginning of the 21st Century], edited by Karel Malý & Michal Tomášek. Praha: Karolinum, 2009, 241.

Articles in Journals

Kříž, Jakub. '*Vliv judikatury Evropského soudu pro lidská práva na náboženskou svobodu v České republice*' [Impact of the Judicature of the European Court of Human Rights on Religious Freedom in the Czech Republic]*Jurisprudence* 7–8 (2012): 37.

Přibyl, Stanislav. '*Pojetí tzv. "zvláštních práv" církví a náboženských společností podle zákona č. 3/2002 Sb*'. [Concept of So-called 'Special Rights' of Churches and Religious Societies According to Act No. 3/2002 Coll.]. *Revue církevního práva [Church Law Review]*: 27 (2004): 7–20.

Selected Bibliography

Šimáčková, Kateřina. '*Ideologická neutralita státu a postavení církví v České republice*' [The Ideological Neutrality of the State and the Position of Churches in the Czech Republic]. *Revue církevního práva [Church Law Review]* 35 (2006): 193–202.
Law Periodicals
Torfs, Rik (ed.). *European Journal for Church and State Research.* Leuven: Peeters, since 1994.
Tretera, Jiří Rajmund (ed.). *Revue církevního práva* [Church Law Review]. Praha: Společnost pro církevní právo, since 1995. Available online at: Church Law Society http://spcp.prf.cuni.cz/1-10/frame.htm

Selected Bibliography

Index

The numbers here refer to paragraph numbers.

Adventists, 20, 45, 158, 211, 243, 259
Affiliation, *see* Religious affiliation
Apostolic Church, *see* Pentecostals
Apostolic See, 35, 50, 58, 130, 132, 134 et seq., 138, 141, 145, 179
Armenians, 20
Associations, 12, 88, 89, 108, 113, 150, 152, 172, 190, 225
Atheism, 15, 19, 41, 61, 83, 128, 252, 289, 291
Asylum, 68, 86, 92
Augsburg Confession, 16, 30
Autonomy, 15, 29, 70, 71, 74, 107, 122 et seq., 182, 190, 196, 198, 210, 262

Baptists, 20, 45, 158, 211, 259
Belief, 56, 77, 78, 81 et seq., 94, 98 et seq., 103, 116, 178, 207, 213, 221, 223, 279
Blasphemy, 222
Blood transfusion, 215
Broadcasting, 175, 289
Buddhism, 18, 20
Buildings, 226, 230, 231, 251, 252, 287, 293

Calvinists, *see* Helvetic Confession
Catholic Church, 29, 33, 36, 46, 72, 83, 130, 144, 145, 153, 158, 167, 170, 171, 229
- Greek, 16, 20, 45, 48, 131, 141, 211
- Roman, 2, 16, 20, 33, 40, 141, 211, 243, 244, 246, 257, 259

Census, 4, 13, 16, 119
Chaplains
- armed forces, 87, 120, 153 et seq.
- hospital, 89, 165 et seq.
- prison, 88, 147, 149 et seq.

Charities, 57, 90, 109, 111, 141, 161, 201, 225, 256
Charter of Fundamental Rights and Freedoms, 8, 55, 60, 75, 76, 81, 92, 98, 101, 102, 104, 106, 124, 125, 127, 181, 193, 206, 209, 210, 216, 241, 291
Children, 4, 32, 46, 47, 78 et seq., 91, 92, 247, 254, 255
Christian Congregations, 20, 211, 245
Christian Fellowship Church, *see* Pentecostals
Church of Brethren, 16, 18, 20, 158, 211, 259
Church tax, 227
Church schools, *see* Religious schools
Clergy, *see* Ministers
Collections, 224 et seq., 239
Communism, 15, 41 et seq., 53, 72, 73, 102, 107, 121, 128, 130, 135, 147, 190, 222, 230, 233, 251, 252, 276
Concordat, 35, 58, 130 et seq., 140 et seq., 179
Confessional secrecy, 211 et seq.
Congregationalists, *see* Church of Brethren
Congrua, 31, 42, 121
Conscientious objection, *see* Objection
Constitution, 1, 8, 31, 32, 48, 55, 57, 60, 85, 100, 124, 129, 193, 272
Contributions, 224, 227, 229, 239
Convents, 134, 228, 230, 231, 251, 252, 293
Criminal, 152, 207, 209, 212, 220, 223
- Code, 68, 74, 212, 222, 223
- Procedure Code, 68

Cultural monuments, 287, 288
Czech Bishops' Conference, 16, 69, 87, 131, 143, 145, 148, 153 et seq., 169, 172, 174, 187
Czechoslovak Hussite Church, 16, 20, 158, 198, 211, 226, 243, 256, 257, 259, 266

Darbists, *see* Christian Congregations
Data protection, 12, 15, 126, 202 et seq.
Diaconias, 90, 109, 111, 161
Dioceses, 2, 67, 111, 131, 135, 141, 227, 244, 251, 252, 252, 264, 268
Domestic agreements, 66, 69, 86, 131, 146, 192
Donations, 224, 225, 227
Due process, 209 et seq.
Dues, 224

Ecumenical Council of Churches in the Czech Republic, 20, 69, 86, 87, 131, 148, 153 et seq., 187
Education, 241 et seq.
Employment, 4, 152, 195, 196, 201, 219, 221, 244
Endowments, 224, 228
European Convention on Human Rights, 9, 177
European Union, 8, 183, 202, 217, 219
Euthanasia, 214
Evangelical Church
  A.C., 5, 20, 117, 131, 211, 243, 259
  of Czech Brethren, 16, 20, 33, 131, 158, 188, 211, 226, 243, 257, 259, 265

Family, 1, 7, 68, 80, 91, 126, 157, 163, 271 et seq., 289, 291
Financing, 144, 194, 224 et seq., 250
First World War, 33
Forced labour units, 44, 74, 126
Forum
  externum, 76
  internum, 75
Freedom of expression, 65, 94, 126, 206 et seq., 293

Greek Catholic, *see* Catholic Church, Greek
Gypsies, *see* Roma

Harassment, 220
Hare Krishna Movement, 18, 20
Hatred, 223, 289
Helvetic Confession, 16, 30, 33
Heritage, *see* Inheritance
Herrnhut Church, *see* Unity of Brethren
Hindu, 18, 20
Holocaust, 67, 232
Holy Roman Empire, 24
Holy See, *see* Apostolic See
Hospital, 90, 164
  see also Chaplains, hospital
Housing, 219

Immigration, 18
Inheritance, 224, 228, 239
International law, 55, 135, 176 et seq.
International treaties, 9, 66, 92, 102, 124, 176 et seq., 202
Intolerance, *see* Hatred
Irvingism, 20, 211
Islam, 20, 191

Jehovah's witnesses, 16, 20, 45, 117, 215, 243
Jews, 20, 36, 37, 187, 190, 232, 257, 259, 266
Judaism *see* Jews

Labour law, 195 et seq.
Lands, 1, 4, 6, 16, 19, 21, 23, 29, 30, 36, 43, 72, 85, 122, 124, 130, 147, 222, 251, 265, 271, 272
Latter-Day Saints, 20, 211
Legal person, 109, 111 et seq., 141, 191, 201, 203, 262
Legal personality, 12, 99, 111 et seq., 141, 262
Lidice, 39
Lutheran Church, *see* Evangelical Church A. C.

Marriage, 4, 43, 120, 141, 205, 271 et seq.
Marxists, 41, 46, 73
Media, 74, 187, 201, 289 et seq.
Medical treatment, 215
Membership, 15, 33, 62, 208, 216, 219
Methodist Church, 20, 158, 211
Military chaplaincy, *see* Chaplains, armed forces
Military service, 63, 87, 95, 141
Military Spiritual Service, 20, 87
Ministers, 87, 135, 141, 149, 159 et seq., 171, 182, 196 et seq., 211, 212, 241

Index

Ministry, 12, 20, 67, 69, 87, 97, 99, 109, 111 et seq., 115, 117, 138, 153 et seq., 158, 161, 163, 180, 240, 243, 248, 257, 259, 270
Modus Vivendi, *see* Concordat
Monasteries, 44, 111, 134, 228, 230, 231, 252, 287, 293
Moravian Brethren, *see* Unity of the Brethren
Mormons, *see* Latter-Day Saints
Municipalities, 10, 31, 85, 184, 241, 242, 250, 291
Munich conference, 40
Muslims, *see* Islam

Nazism, 36, 53, 190, 274
Neutrality, 70, 291
New Apostolic Church, *see* Irvingism
Non-discrimination, 216 et seq.
Nuremberg Laws, 36

Objection, 93 et seq., 213, 214
Old Catholic Church, 20, 158, 211, 266
Orthodox Church, 5, 16, 20, 33, 39, 158, 211

Parents, 78, 79, 215, 247, 274
Parish, 5, 36, 39, 111, 148, 230, 246, 251, 287
Parity, 31, 70, 71, 118, 128, 130
Parliament, 9, 10, 28, 54 et seq., 58, 109, 135, 138, 176, 193, 194, 217, 219, 233, 278, 202
Penal law, 222 et seq.
Pentecostals, 20, 158, 211, 243, 259
Petition, 51, 126, 293
Plymouth Brethren, *see* Christian Congregations
Police, 15, 53, 83, 146, 159 et seq., 292
Political parties, 34, 186, 190
Practice of religion, 86, 92
Preamble, 1, 125, 233
Presbyterian, 16, 33
Priests, 25, 31, 33, 36, 38, 39, 49, 147, 252, 264, 266, 268, 269
Prison, 147 et seq.
Prisoner, 88, 147
Privacy, 126, 202 et seq.
Private schools, 120, 247 et seq., 255
Proceeds from property, 224, 229
Property, 42, 59, 62, 67, 74, 121, 126, 144, 193, 194, 216, 224, 228 et seq., 250
Property settlement, 59, 67, 74, 121, 187, 193, 194, 224, 233, 236, 237, 293
Protestants, 5, 7, 25, 28 et seq., 33, 38, 45, 49, 172, 175, 189, 257, 265
Public debate, 278, 293
Public sphere, 131

Reformation, 25, 132
Reformed Church, *see* Helvetic Confession
Registered religious community, 11, 12, 16, 20, 87, 89, 108, 111 et seq., 119, 173, 239, 240
Registered unions of religious communities, 111, 112
Registration, 12, 13, 58, 100, 112 et seq., 151, 183, 244, 260, 280, 281
  two-degree, 58, 116 et seq.
Religious affiliation, 14, 31, 85, 253
Religious education, 32, 46, 47, 63, 91, 92, 120, 142, 241 et seq.
Religious schools, 225, 231, 247 et seq., 287
Restitution, *see* Property settlement
Right not to believe, 85
Right to assemble, 65
Right to associate, 65, 126
Ritual slaughter, 97
Roma, 4, 7
Roman Catholic, *see* Catholic Church, Roman

Salvation Army, 20
Schools, *see* Religious schools
Second World War, 4, 40
Separation, 31, 71, 109
Social care, 141
Socialism, *see* Communism
Special rights, 57, 115 et seq., 191, 242, 259, 280
State neutrality towards religion, *see* Neutrality
State's permission, 42, 54, 83, 115, 246
State symbols, 2
Subsidies, 31, 42, 121, 234, 237, 288
Suicide, 214

Tax, 238 et seq.
see also Church tax
Teachers, 244, 252, 253, 256, 266, 268, 269
Tenancy, 230, 231
Testamentary succession, 228
Theological schools, 40, 45, 66, 142, 260 et seq.
Toleration, 30
Treaty, 26
see also International treaties
Te Deum, 291

Unions of Religious Communities, 20, 111 et seq.
Unitarians, 20, 211, 266
Universities, 24, 25, 36, 53, 142, 157, 226, 244, 255, 256, 260 et seq.
United Nations, 8, 124, 178
Unity of the Brethren (Moravian Brethren), 20, 27, 158

Vatican City, 135, 138, 179
Victimization, 220
Volyn Czechs, 5

Worship, 33, 74, 76, 109, 225

Zelów, 5

www.ingramcontent.com/pod-product-compliance
Lightning Source LLC
Chambersburg PA
CBHW071351230926
51846CB00002B/508
* 9 7 8 9 0 4 1 1 8 7 5 5 0 *